Bazaar

·BOOK OF·

SOFT FURNISHINGS

or '12/93 *
sec'

~ *Acknowledgements* ~

My very grateful thanks to the following people, all of whom contributed splendidly
towards the success of this book and series:
Suzanne Webber, Susan Martineau,
Frank Phillips, Jennie Allen, Sarah Amit and Laura Smith at
BBC Books, and to Wendy Hobson and Kate Simunek;
Erica Griffiths, Anne O'Dwyer, Jane Fletcher, Chris Homan,
Roger Parris and the *Bazaar* team at BBC Television;
Merchandise Information Office at the John Lewis Partnership;
Miles O'Donovan and Susan Hogg at Material World;
Ian Mankin at Ian Mankin Ltd;
Wendi Dellanegra and Debbie Harris;
and lastly, my husband Rod Parker.

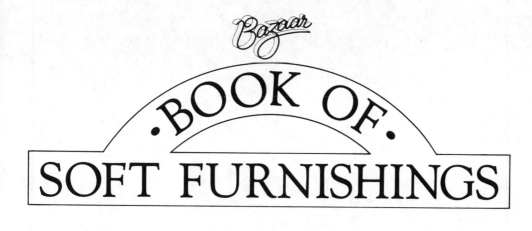

Bazaar
·BOOK OF·
SOFT FURNISHINGS

CHARMIAN WATKINS

BBC BOOKS

This book is published to accompany a series of programmes prepared in consultation with the BBC Broadcasting Council.

Published by BBC Books
a division of BBC Enterprises Limited,
Woodlands, 80 Wood Lane, London W12 0TT
First published 1990
© Charmian Watkins 1990
ISBN 0 563 36026 7
Illustrations pages 7–36 © Kate Simunek 1990
All other illustrations © Charmian Watkins 1990
Set in 11/13 pt Perpetua Roman
by Ace Filmsetting Ltd, Frome, Somerset
Printed and bound in Great Britain by Richard Clay Ltd, Norwich & Bungay
Cover printed by Richard Clay Ltd, Norwich

~ Contents ~

Introduction

I was very excited when I was asked to write this book. It was a chance to show not only how easy it is to create successful and professional-looking soft furnishings with total confidence, but to encourage everyone to look again through fresh eyes at what they already have around the home.

People are often nervous about tackling what they consider is the domain of the professional. All that gloss and expense surely cannot be done at home? Don't I have to use expensive fabrics, own fabulous furniture and gloriously proportioned rooms to achieve that special 'look'? Well, the answer is no. With just a little basic knowhow, your results could well be a lot more exciting and fresher than those of people who do it for a living.

I began designing when I was a near-penniless music student. Obviously I could not afford to buy the simple and chic clothes I longed for in expensive boutiques. Have you noticed that the simpler the design, the more expensive it tends to be? So I began sewing my own clothes, buying fabric when and where I could and, before long, friends were asking me to make 'doubles' for them. From there a totally different career snowballed from the one for which I was trained. From singing the odd Messiah I developed a manufacturing business supplying top shops here and abroad with my designs. I wrote three fashion books, which included patterns and instructions for making clothes at home, followed by *Decorating with Fabric Liberty Style*, again with instructions for recreating the designs featured.

Having been slightly overawed by the sleek finish of designed interiors to begin with, I soon found that soft furnishings were a lot easier than clothing, and much more fun. You cannot really go out in a jacket with one sleeve missing, but you can throw a length of fabric over a tatty old sofa and leave it there for a few months until you've decided what to do with it. So, let's break through the mystique surrounding interior design created by all designers, myself included, and pass it on to everyone. All you really need is confidence.

There are very few rules and regulations regarding interiors or soft furnishing. Most design ideas are coloured by practical considerations. Is the room very small or too tall for its size? A small room with a high ceiling can be made to look more comfortable by adding a wallpaper or stencilled border at, for example, picture rail height. Or you could add a dado rail or wooden moulding strip at chair-back height to divide the walls in two using a deeper shading beneath the dado. You could also experiment with deeper valances to top curtains, but the main trick here is to cut the height.

A low ceiling can be very claustrophobic and needs careful thought to heighten it. Light shades of colour should be used to create a feeling of airiness. Keep walls 'uncut' horizontally, taking the same shade of wall from ceiling to skirting board. Avoid borders which will pull the room down – heavy valances will do nothing to help the height of the room, so keep curtain shapes simple and try to draw the eye to chair and table-lamp height by using brighter colours against the paler background to create interest. Cushions in yellows, gold, peach and red heaped on creamy coloured chairs will attract the eye.

Apart from disguising problems of ceiling height you may want to make a room more welcoming, comfortable, cosy or larger – all these considerations are tackled daily by professionals. What they, and you, need to do is work out a brief. Given the basics of your problem or plan, you set out to solve and improve on the original. The real point is that you should enjoy yourself, since this feeling will transfer itself to the room you are working on. It is also absolutely possible to achieve your plan within your own budget, whatever that may be. It is very easy to spend a fortune making a room look good but it is much cleverer to do it inexpensively!

All over the country there are outlets selling really beautiful fabrics much more cheaply than you would imagine. Several shops make a policy of not charging more than a certain amount for their stock, which they obtain as end-of-runs or in special deals passed on to the shopper. Other good sources include markets, sales, house sales and auctions. And of course a fresh eye applied to existing furnishings or fabrics can result in surprising new ideas. Many people have the odd length of fabric which they've tucked away meaning to 'do something with it' sooner or later. Have a look in the back of your cupboard or attic and I can guarantee you'll be amazed at your findings. Take it all out and heap it into piles of matching tones, all red hues together, for example. See what goes with what. Would it now be a good idea to lengthen those too-short plain curtains with something a little brighter in a small print? And what about a valance to hide ugly curtain pleating? You could use a similarly coloured print for making a tablecloth which will pull the room together.

When putting different fabrics together, be careful to match weights. A heavy edging on light-weight fabric will simply pull at stitching lines. And floaty organza will be useless lovingly bound around the edges of heavy velvet curtains where damask-type fabrics, which are firmer and more densely woven, could be used successfully. Don't forget that a lighter fabric can always be plumped-up by interlining between the main curtain fabric and lining. As a general rule when choosing interlining, remember to match the weight of the main fabric. Mixing textures can also give really interesting results as long as fabric weights more or less match, so think about the practicalities and then have a go.

Carry around a piece of card and, as you collect snippets of the sort of colours and fabrics you like, pin them to this to see if you are happy with the effect they create together. (Professionals always do this and I call it a storyboard.) Try the new colours out on a little sketch of your room coloured in with pencils. Have you got the balance of light and shade right? How could you brighten up the room, add a new colour or take one away, regroup pictures or tart up an old frame to add lustre? Look at glossy magazines in the library to find the type of style you like. Don't be put off by obviously expensive trappings. It is much more chic to be low-key! Analyse the furnishings, see what colours have been mixed, whether the effect is warm and welcoming or cold and unfriendly, where lights have been placed for best effect or where a badly plastered wall has been disguised by stencilling or wallpaper. Two or three cushions can transform a room – lifting a colour from curtains for a deeper-shaded cushion, or using up an unworn section of old rug for cushion covers.

Take an evening course in something which particularly interests you. Lacquering, for example, picture framing, paint finishes or lampshades. You can always swap finished items with a friend or give them as presents.

Creativity is not the prerogative of the rich. It belongs to all of us and innovation is the tool we use to realise it. If you adore red, use it toned down to terracotta to begin with and turn a dark din-ing-room into a warm, inviting place. Look out for old velvet curtains at jumble sales to provide luxury and warmth. When they're cleaned and edged with braid in a deeper tone of brick-red no one will notice if they're a little worn. The fabric is sure to be better quality than most of what is available now. Add your favourite red in little touches to begin with, building up slowly to achieve a balance with which you will be happy. Keep the shades of colour you use close to create a subtle effect. Sometimes just adding piping in a stronger tone of red to cushions or chairs will provide sufficient accent, but one or two deep yellow cushions and yellow lampshades could add a necessary edge to the overall look of the room. And what about a rude shade of pink as the perfect full-stop? Tear out the sort of look you are after from a magazine and carry it around with your room sketch and storyboard until you find the right bargain or can do a good swap with a friend.

Narrow wallpaper borders are inexpensive and can look very special when used to decorate a boring wooden picture frame.

It really is a fallacy to think that unless you own particularly beautiful furniture, chairs or pictures a designed look cannot be yours. Some of the most successful interiors are just that because they remove the clutter and concentrate on the essence of the room, using only one or two items as focal points. Chairs can be covered with throws, furniture, floors and walls painted and small amounts of fabric and colour used to best effect in areas where they show the most, in cushions for example. Providing you are disciplined about your use of colour when opting for this cool, clean approach and you position lighting carefully, the results can be stunning. For those of us on limited budgets a minus can very easily be turned into a plus.

Rooms are living things. My home is by no means perfect. My sitting-room walls need decorating, the small tables (actually ugly speakers topped with fibreboard circles) are draped with remnants of fabric to help me decide if I like the colour combination of black with yellow. They have been there a year and I am still waiting for the sales. Nothing needs to be done at once. Take your time. Let your ideas grow and develop as you experiment – this is meant to give you pleasure.

Instructions for making up most of the soft furnishing ideas mentioned here are given in the following pages together with a few simple techniques. I have made the sewing processes as straightforward as possible so that even beginners can achieve the effects shown, whilst giving you the opportunity to achieve professional finishes. You will also find a useful list of countrywide suppliers at the back of the book.

Create a relaxing sitting-room

Now let's talk specifics. The sitting-room should, as its name suggests, be a room in which you enjoy relaxing. A feeling of space is important here and light, airy, summery rooms can be made from quite plain ones by the use of a fresh colour such as yellow. If you can face repainting the room, do it. For example, a darker yellow on walls which is then picked up by curtains of a lighter background in a chintz of yellow, apricot, brick red and dark green foliage, perhaps edged in green to tie in with an existing dark green sofa, would look wonderful if those colours continue to be repeated throughout the room. You really want to

Add a matching valance to existing curtains, extending this length with plain
fabric matching the valance binding and curtain print. Add shaped tiebacks and
cushions to match and decorate the wall with a toning wallpaper border, finishing
off with a floppy picture bow.

aim for a balance between light and shade. All light or all dark colourings create a flat, boring effect which has no life to it. It's like looking at a page of print with no paragraphs or full stops. Colours should give a balance between dark and light, creating a look that is airy but also has bite to it. They really can be made to work to your advantage.

Begin by taking one existing favourite item in your sitting-room and then building on it: a rug or sofa, for example, or even something as small as a cushion or tablecloth. Add a print with light and dark shades to complement the colour of this item and develop those colours into curtains and valances, binding the edges with one of the colours in the print. If your curtains are plain, freshen them up by making a border for them in a print containing the curtain colour. Make a fixed, bound-edged valance to match, setting it on a wooden pelmet above the existing track. There is no need to cover the pelmet since it will not be visible. Or, you could set a pole above the curtain track and buy a length of material in a toning colour or print, and then line it and edge it in bullion fringing along one long side. Then loosely drape this over the pole so the ends hang as tails down each outer side of the curtains. Tiebacks could then be made from the same fabric, bound or piped in the curtain colouring.

Use any left-over fabric for cushion covers, differently frilled or piped in the same binding colour, then add more scatter cushions in plain, interestingly textured fabrics using the colours in the print. They could have a simple frilled edge, a bound and frilled edge, be double-frilled, sport piping or bought braid, be made with Oxford borders, be buttoned, gathered into piping at plump corners – any combination is possible and I'll explain how to tackle them all! They could even be quilted or appliquéd.

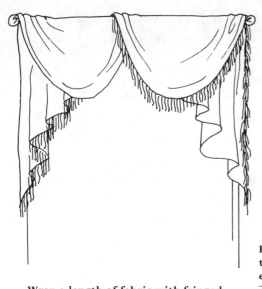

Wrap a length of fabric with fringed edging around a pole for a really dramatic effect.

Hook a shaped tieback against the wall to hold back curtains and pipe its edges to match.

Cushions provide unending opportunities to emphasise other trimmings and colours in a room, to provide the all-important 'full stop'. Their colour alone can transform a boring sofa into an inviting one and they are very easy and inexpensive to make. Use old cushion pads or feather eiderdowns for stuffing, but for goodness' sake don't cut the eiderdown before you have stitched around the shape you require with two rows of stitching, cutting between the rows, or the room will look like a henhouse.

Make use of little tables set with table-lamps beside chairs where possible, to give good reading light. Use old quilted bed-spreads of toning colours, or other heavyweight fabric to cover them to the floor. Or make circular tablecloths of a smaller print but in matching colours to the curtains, bound to match the other furnishings. You could interline wider bindings to create a plump, rounded bottom edge to a tablecloth, giving it an air of importance. It is also useful to throw fabric of related colours over the worn arms of old easy chairs which need new covers. At least they are now the correct colour for the room and you have time to consider what fabric to choose when you do have the money and/or the time to get the job done.

Be careful in your choice of mixed prints. It is actually quite difficult to achieve a relaxed, informal yet 'together' look with several different prints. Choose one main print you feel you can live with for years, add another smaller print of the same nature. For example you could team a classic English nineteenth-century design in chintz with a small sprig pattern and edge both in plain chintz. A simple check could be added should another pattern be required. Fabric pattern books often suggest co-ordinated prints which make life easier. It may sound boring advice to give to those of you choosing new fabric, but you are much more likely to tire of a vivid, fashion-conscious design than of a more classical one. Better to add those adventurous touches in small areas which you can change as time goes by, rather than by overdoing the trendy approach, only to hate it all in five years' time. It is also often far more effective to use only one print, particularly with chintzes as these often have busy designs using several colours which can lose their overall effect and look muddled if used with other prints. Chintz has a lovely light, airy feel to it but the fabric should be used generously. If you can't afford to do this, it is much better to use mainly cheaper, plain fabrics of different interesting textures, and use a more expensive print that you love where it will show the most; in cushion covers or on a screen, for instance, and where less is needed.

Some fabrics, such as striped and checked moires, are specifically designed to be used together and will be displayed together in shops. In this case half the work is done for you and you can have fun planning what will go where. Don't forget how effective a plain border can be, pulling out one of the stronger colours of a print. And it is cheaper to use fabric edgings which you have cut yourself than to apply metres of bought braid or fringing.

Look carefully at the arrangement of chairs in the room. Can they be turned round to face each other more happily? Does everyone sit in a row when visiting you? Try to make the arrangement a comfortable one for chatting, then position lighting carefully near chairs and in corners, where possible, to make the room seem larger. Make softly pleated or plain, stiffened paper lampshades in pale, warm colours such as pink or cream and edge them with velvet or braid. Carefully choose the colours to complement those in the room and use the central overhead light as little as possible – it creates a hard, tiring effect.

If you don't have to worry about small children or pets knocking them flying, the tables on which you set your lamps are also perfect for displaying groups of favourite objects. I have a 'thing' for carved wooden frogs, but you may love china cats or be collecting small bottles in shades which go together. A collection of driftwood pieces would look lovely with an arrangement of dried flowers and grasses in the same colours behind them. Favourite pieces of china could be carefully displayed so you can enjoy them. Put the largest objects towards the back and group other items around it. Imagine you have taken a photograph of the arrangement and its background. Does it make a pleasing picture in itself? Is it balanced? Does it look interesting?

If you only have a few pictures you can make a stronger effect grouping these together too. You could make a picture bow or two for a special frame or to tie two similar frames together. For such a small amount of fabric you might use a silk remnant plumped up with interlining for maximum effect, possibly in a strong, related colour to add interest to a plain wall, letting the bow sit proud of the wall about 25cm (10in) above the picture and its tails drape naturally behind the chosen picture to fall the same length below the frame. This is also a very effective way to add height to a room when it is needed.

Walls too can be made more interesting by painting them with one of the special paint effects such as stippling or colourwashing. Stippling involves going over fresh brushwork with a soft wad of cloth to create a grainy look, while for colourwashing, a natural-colour undercoat is applied to existing wall colour with curved brush strokes to create a brushed effect through which the original colour glows. These effects are very exciting and often much cheaper than applying wallpaper. You could try putting a pale shade of paint onto white or pastel walls using a brush with long hairs (called a flogger) and applying a coat of flat varnish afterwards for an antique, dragged look. A stippling brush will give a speckled look or you could use little sponges for a different, mottled effect. Look up the various techniques in a specialist paint book from the library and experiment using sample pots or left-over paint. For small rooms with high ceilings, paint walls in two shades of the same colour, divided at chair-back height by a stencilled or bought wallpaper border. The darker colour would go beneath the border and any woodwork could be painted two or three shades lighter than the walls for emphasis. The same treatment of woodwork could be used for low-ceilinged rooms, but walls should be left in one colour only and ceilings should be very pale to add height to the room.

Borders at ceiling height also give a softened and finished effect, though they can lower the ceiling further if it is already low. Alternatively, use borders around skirting-board height, taking them up and over door and window frames for a very finished, decorative look. Wallpaper, not always a more expensive option, can be very effective in hiding badly plastered or old walls, and tiny, one-colour woodcut prints in small bedrooms can look charming. Be careful, though, of using a very small print in a larger room. It can disappear to give only a textured look, something you could possibly achieve more cheaply by the different paint finishes available. If this is already the case, you might improve the 'drowned' effect by adding a co-ordinated border to lift and strengthen the design. Lots of wallpaper manufacturers are producing these now (and not just the expensive ones) so look around. You would then need sharper coloured or larger printed soft furnishings to add depth and character to the room, allowing the wallpaper to act purely as background.

Make an unfriendly dining-room more inviting

Take a dark, north-facing dining-room: dark, mahogany table and chairs circa 1930 with dark brown sideboard. It's cold and uninviting and you always need the light on. Think about what you want to use the room for. If it is simply for eating in and because it is so unfriendly you tend to eat in the kitchen or on your knee in the sitting-room, then you are wasting a room you could transform into one which is warm and inviting. Begin by

Join two skimpy curtains to form one luxurious drape to one side of a narrow
window, catching it back with a heavily tasselled tieback. Add a lacquer-framed
fabric screen to decorate a dark corner and sew a matching bound tablecloth,
dropped-in chair seats and chairback covers in toning shades. Stencilled walls and
a lacquer paper lampshade add further depth to create a warm
and welcoming interior.

forgetting to try to lighten the room. It does not always work and, anyway, the centre of the dining-room is its table. This is where the light emphasis should be. Warm the rest of the room with deep colours to make it more cosy. Keep a warmly patterned tablecloth always in place and cover this with a plain cloth when the table is in use. Get the lighting right: it should be at eye level, not at ceiling height if you want to enjoy your friends' faces and make them feel comfortable and cared for. No friend of mine would give me more shadows under my eyes than I already have. So cap off the central ceiling light fitting and forget it. Use table-lamps instead for everyday eating boosted by candles at the table for special evenings. For next to nothing you can make lampshades from stiffened paper (available from art shops) in darker, more exotic colours which will throw light downwards to create a warm, intimate glow. Revamp the old frame of an unloved shade of the right shape to save buying another frame. Nor need lamp bases be a problem. Use old baskets repainted in gloss paint, turned upside down and installed with brass lamp fittings purchased from any DIY store. Or make a wooden box and paint it using an ordinary emulsion marbled with fine veins of lighter colours applied in a criss-cross fashion and fidgeted to blend the edges. Then varnish to finish, before fixing the fitting.

If you like the 'antique look', paint mismatched furniture in similar shades of emulsion for a matt, faded look which produces a dragged effect.

Screens used to be employed for purely practical reasons to stop draughts from badly fitting doors or windows or to hide a serving hatch or handbasin. They can still be found in junk shops for very little outlay and are very effective for sub-dividing a too-large room or one that is used for two different purposes, such as dividing study and bedroom area. Nowadays their use is often simply decorative. They can be used very successfully in dark, dreary corners to create interest and colour and are an exciting way to display favourite fabrics or holiday snaps. I've designed one for you to make which is very easily put together. Use the same gloss or lacquer paint as on the lamp bases to paint the outer frames of the screen, covering it with a glowing tapestry-like fabric for really luxurious effect. It can then be backed with plain lining fabric for economy.

Look closely at your dining-room chair seats. Could they do with recovering? It might be very effective to use fabrics of the same colours and print sizes, but just slightly different designs, for a harlequin effect. In this case bin-ends at sales are the per-

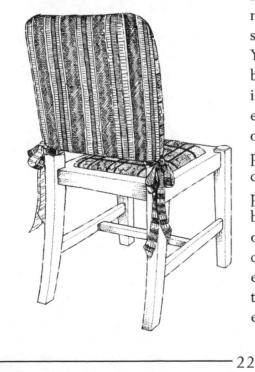

fect hunting ground for the odd metre. Why not use moire stripes for a stronger effect? You could also cover ugly chair backs in the same way by making slips of the same fabrics, all edged and tied at the base in one colour to pull the different prints together. A tablecloth could also be made in one of the prints, edged in decorative braid. Drape the tablecloth onto the floor if you can, to create a more relaxed and more elegant finish. Again, you are trying to add warmth and interest in matched colours.

If the overall effect still does not seem quite warm enough, go the whole hog and redecorate the walls in warm brick, stencilling around their tops at ceiling height with shades of the other colours used in the room. You can make your own stencils very inexpensively. They take a little time to apply but the results can be stunning, adding interest to plain walls and helping to create a softened mood. And since you are redecorating walls why not rearrange pictures, setting them together in an overall square or rectangle shape, larger ones at the top if there is room and smaller ones just above eye level so, when you are seated, they can be more easily enjoyed. Postcards, theatre programmes or posters are just some of the pictures you might like to mount. A collage of holiday snaps cut around and set into one larger frame makes the difference between taking them out once a year and being able to enjoy them constantly. Family photographs set in small frames and grouped together into an overall design look as good on the wall as arranged on mantlepiece or sideboard. Frames of different sizes look much more interesting when grouped together. Clean up old frames and transform badly damaged or boring ones by repainting. New picture frames tend to be expensive, so try junk shops or jumbles for old, damaged frames which can be renewed with a little love. I always have far more pictures to hang than I have frames, so I am constantly on the look-out for a bargain.

As an alternative to pictures, try displaying old china or modern pottery plates in small collections on the wall with plate racks or hangers.

How to handle a hall

Halls often get a lot of heavy wear, particularly from children, prams, pushchairs and the like. If you live in an older house with dado rails in the hall, it might be both useful and interesting to apply anaglypta wallpaper under the dado, covering it with a washable gloss or semi-gloss paint so it can be easily sponged free of the results of sticky fingers and toy car wheels. My two-year-old bounces himself diagonally along our hall walls as if incapable of making his way unaided. Short of shouting at him every time he comes to see me in the kitchen, the best answer is to apply washable paint: much nicer for both of us and good to look at. Alternatively you could apply a washable wallpaper border or stencilling at the same height, repainting below it and taking the border up the stairs to include the landing. The border could be continued around doors and windows too. If you live in a modern house or flat with lower ceilings, your hall might look better with plainer painted or wallpapered walls lifted by painting the woodwork two shades lighter than the walls.

If your landing or hall is dark, as in so many houses, why not try to find an old mirror – it does not really matter if the silvering has 'gone home' at the corners – in a second-hand shop or saleroom which you can place at the top of the stairs or opposite a light source, to double the amount of light. New mirrors can be expensive to buy, but older ones often have lovely decorative details in the frame which create added interest on a plain wall. Revamp the frame by painting it perhaps with metallic or coach paint. It is amazing what a mirror can do not only to make a room seem much larger than it really is by reflecting its view, but to increase light anywhere there is a dark area. If you use unframed mirror glass, unless you plan to frame it with, for example, wooden mouldings available from any large timber merchant, try to cover a complete wall for best effect. I saw this done years ago in a dark basement hallway. Plants placed in front of the mirror had doubled in thickness and there seemed to be twice as many pictures as were actually there; it was so effective that everyone kept bumping into each other since we had all overestimated the amount of space.

A large mirror can sometimes seem daunting set on its own in a hallway or on a landing. One way of creating a picture around it is to set a small, narrow table in front of the mirror on which is placed a simple vase of fresh or dried flowers or an arrangement of favourite bits and bobs. Perhaps you possess a stripped pine table of just the right size. Interestingly, pine was originally considered undressed if not painted, and was usually covered in decorative paintwork much of which has been lost because of the fashion for stripping down to the wood. Now that the fashion for painted furniture as it was originally conceived is returning, why not paint and stencil a simple, inexpensive table to suit your own colour scheme. Or if you don't want to 'attack' your favourite pine table, try painting and stencilling an old veneered table or cupboard that has seen better days. Yes, it will take time, but many of these techniques are not difficult to achieve and imagine the satisfaction when you have finished. Why not try evening classes for a crash course?

Although dados, skirting boards, picture rails and door surrounds are more often than not painted white, there is a lot to be said for having these in a deeper colour, especially where a stronger, more modern look is required. And don't forget that the cheapest way of revamping flooring is by painting the floorboards. Using colours which compliment those already there can create stunning effects. Be careful though about too dark a colour for woodwork. Darker shades can draw the hall in, making it look even smaller than it already is.

Have fun in the bedroom!

Bedrooms are often the perfect excuse to let all fantasies fly. They could be transformed into a souk with Moroccan rugs and wall-hangings; become a gloriously flowery garden with an easily made four-poster bed-frame painted and hung with curtains and valances; or simplified with a cool blue and white check used throughout the room. Many of the fabrics available are very feminine and it can be a mistake to overdo the frilly approach. My husband hates this look, so I have to be careful to use prints which are not too fussy. Oriental prints in darker colours such as black and lacquer red give a more mysterious look to a bedroom, while paisleys, checks or abstract designs are good alternatives to frills and flowers.

If using a print, particularly a chintz, it is a good idea to stick to the one design throughout, since it will give a much stronger, less random look to the room. Use the print to edge or make curtains, tiebacks, valances and bedspread, edging them with a plain colour for a really finished look. Odd covers can be used to disguise ugly bedside tables and these could in turn be covered with smaller fine white tea-table cloths, for example of the type that can be picked up in junk shops for very little, or fished out of gran's bottom drawer. A length of lace, proper or synthetic, looks lovely thrown over a patterned cloth, but don't overdo the lace unless you want a boudoir. Walls could be given one of the specialist paint finishes I have described earlier or covered in a tiny sprig design wallpaper or a fine shirting stripe which may be more acceptable to frill-haters. Try a narrow border around the tops and bottoms of walls for a pretty finish.

Beds these days tend to be set much lower than they used to be, drawing the eye downwards and leaving a lot of wall space exposed to create a wide, uneasy-looking gap all round the room

Transform the blank walls of a bedroom with a half-tester suspended high above
the bed, caught back with bow tiebacks. Re-upholster the bedhead and recover
scatter cushions in the same and contrasting prints and add a lined,
bound-edged bedspread to match.

which is difficult to fill. Raise your bed if possible and make it the centre of your room by dressing it attractively. Quilted or patchwork bedcovers are actually very fiddly to make using a domestic sewing machine. They have to be quilted in strips narrow enough to fit under the needle, then sewn together and lined – rather a labour of love. Why not make a simple lined bedspread in printed fabric edged with one of the print colours and make a matching valance, the centre of which can be sewn using an old sheet or similar fabric, since this area will be covered by the mattress? Scatter cushions in various shapes in the same and contrasting fabrics, edged with a matching plain colour would add to the look.

Make the bed more interesting by adding a tester or corona 'headdress' which will also create wall interest. This is lined fabric hung centrally over the bed from the wall behind to drape

This pole end cover finishes off perfectly the gathering of the tester onto its centrally fixed pole above the bed.

The bow tiebacks here have contrast-bound edges for maximum effect, yet are quick and easy to make.

each side, where it is hooked or tied back with bows or cord. It is usually made in the same way as a single curtain, with lots of gathering, then drawn up on its heading so it hangs to each side and around the back of the bed from a central semi-circular or right-angled point. It can look pretty lined with contrasting fabric such as cotton netting. If you drape or gather the 'headdress' from a central fabric-covered pole fixed at right angles to the wall so the fabric falls each side of the bed, it uses much less fabric while still creating the same effect. The fabric will not then drape around the bedhead but with a headboard this will hardly be noticeable. I'll be describing this method later on in the book – it's not as complicated as it sounds. Once you follow the step-by-step instructions, everything falls into place and this is a particularly easy item to make, to maximum effect! The point is to add height to the bed, drawing the eye upwards to create a more balanced room.

The headboard, too, could be recovered in the same fabric. Re-upholstering can be achieved without too much difficulty if the headboard is in bad condition and for details you should refer to specialist upholstery books in the library. But most headboards only need recovering for a total transformation. Set small tables at each side of the bed and cover them with table-cloths draped onto the floor for a softer look, and perhaps bound in the same plain edging as the bed coverings. Use pale shades on bedside lamps for good reading light.

If you can manage new curtains, wonderful. They could be simply gathered for a more relaxed look matching the tester. If you already have long curtains which will complement the colours of the print chosen, try adding bow tiebacks and a fixed valance with gathered heading in the same print with plain binding as before. This will help to pull the look of the room together. A blanket box covered with a cloth or length of fabric could be set at the foot of the bed for the full traditional effect. Even an old tea chest on its side would do.

A much simpler look could be achieved by painting the bedroom in deep cream, all the woodwork a few shades darker and placing the bed in the middle of the room, covered in white bedlinen to create the focal point. A natural-coloured calico roller or Roman blinds, a piece of calico thrown over a chair and deep cream, painted wooden floorboards would create a peaceful, uncluttered room which, with one or two modern light fittings on walls and behind the bed, would look clean and light. Sheets and duvet covers are often at their crispest in plain white. Simple pillowslips could be edged with braid or lace trimming in white or cream to add interest and a white valance made out of the outside, unworn edges of old white sheets. A large wall-hanging or picture in pale shades completes the look. You will find all these ideas explained in detail later on.

For a totally different and more exotic approach use an Oriental print or two. Then imagine a red and beige print with a black background made into curtains and bedspread, reversing to red background print featuring black and beige for the bed valance; deep lacquer-red walls, rugs in the same hues and plain lacquer-red bedside tablecloths, or ones made from old maroon-coloured velvet curtains for bedside tables. Depending on how ambitious you feel, you could make table-lamps out of Chinese ginger jars (eat the ginger first) fitted with red shiny paper lampshades. I've described how to make these later on in the book. Gilt picture frames which have seen better days could be rubbed with a metallic cream to brighten them and then hung in overall square or rectangular designs on the opposite wall. And don't forget how successful a screen can look set in an empty corner and covered in toning fabric for added decoration. If the print colour scheme used features a blue background, you could paint the ceiling a dull, dark blue and set it with stencilled silver stars. Sounds terrible? I've seen it done and it was magical.

Cheering up a child's room

Children's rooms are obviously going to get more cluttered than most. I have found it helps to decorate a room in a mid-tone plain background colour such as harebell blue or daffodil yellow and to choose similar shades in bedclothes, curtains and chair coverings. In a small room this has the advantage of making the space seem larger as well as being more fun than the usual pastels. The teddy bear, duck or rabbit borders you decorated your baby's room with can always be replaced with a border featuring the child's latest interest as he or she grows. It is often said that children will insist on bright colours in their bedrooms, but my son will not sleep when too much is 'going on', so mid-tone blues with just touches of yellow, green and pink have proved much more successful as a background, particularly in making the room seem larger than it actually is.

When choosing curtain material, try to pick a print which will cover as many years as possible. Cuddly teddy bears, sweet as they may be, are not really appropriate for teenagers! What about checks or a more abstract design which will last longer? Line inexpensive wicker baskets with matching fabric to make handy places to store nappies, cleaning equipment and teddies. Tidy away toys in more baskets or matching plastic stacking boxes to save space. Paint a small shelving unit in the same tones and set it on the floor so your child can store his toys and favourite bedtime books where he can get at them. Use the same coloured paint on simple picture frames into which you can fit photographs of lorries, tractors, dolls and teddy bears taken from magazines or postcards. Left-over rectangles of your chosen fabric can be bias bound, set with ties at each end and stitched with cut-out felt rabbits, trains and buses to be hung as a frieze which can be changed as the child grows.

A further use for left-over fabric from a baby's bedroom could be to quilt the print onto 2oz polyester wadding in a simple shoulder-bag shape of the type used to house nappy-changing equipment. Lined with plastic sheeting, possibly with a zip compartment for creams and with a firmly stitched shoulder strap, this could be a very cheap alternative to those found in the shops. Why not edge the bag in contrasting fabric and add further bags to complete the matching collection?

Softening a harsh kitchen

Turning to the kitchen, one often forgets that hard-looking rooms can be softened by the use of fabric which is also useful in pulling together the design of what can be a very untidy room. The problem with most small kitchens is storage space. Analyse what you make most use of in the kitchen and try to store those items in containers of the same type. Some jam jars have very pretty raised designs on them or are interestingly shaped. Wash them out and cover the lids with a circle of printed fabric in one colour to match the rest of the kitchen, cut with pinking shears and gathered in with elastic to fit. Stick a label in the same colour on the front and you have an attractive 'set' of containers.

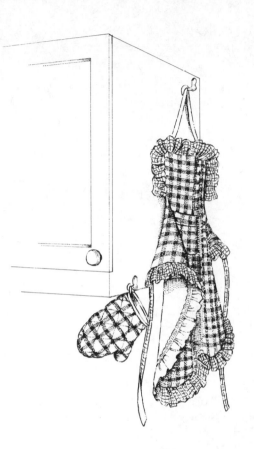

Use the same print to make squab cushions with frilled or piped edges for mismatched chairs, tablecloths, napkins, quilted tablemats and oven gloves. Edge all the quilted items in the same colour bias binding.

Make PVC squab cushions and tablecloth for the kitchen
if you have young children.

A checked café curtain with contrast frilling matches squab cushions with ties for a softer, brighter look to a cold kitchen. Matching, contrast-bound quilted tablemats and new cupboard door handles in toning colour strengthen the effect.

A café curtain with frilled edges will disguise an ugly kitchen window without using as much fabric as full length curtains. You could use the same idea to cover the windows of cupboards and back doors, suspending them at top and bottom on wire. Change the knobs on plain formica cupboard doors to match and paint the café curtain pole and all other woodwork the same or paler shade as the colour of the print. You could even stencil those cupboard doors with a design to go with the print, repeating the stencilling in border form around the kitchen walls above tile level or at ceiling height.

Line the insides of cupboards or recesses where you have open shelving with patterned wallpaper or a darker shade of paint to form an interesting background for plates, cups and saucers and other china.

Old wooden cupboard doors which are unmatched will look far nicer painted in, for example, a dragging technique, then stencilled and covered with a thin layer of varnish to protect them. Use colours such as faded blues and greens or shades of sand and cream, or terracotta shades with darker floorboards painted and covered with two layers of polyurethane varnish so they are well protected. It looks very expensive, takes a little time but costs very little. Eat fast food until the floor dries – your children will love it. For a faded, expensive-looking effect, you could paint modern veneered wooden doors with stains specially produced for this purpose. Try out a small pot of paint on a piece of scrap wood first to be sure you like the results. Greens and greys are particularly effective.

Old, conical 'school' lights can be repainted the original
forest green and hung above the kitchen table on a longer
flex to give good reading and working light. They can be
found in junk shops and jumbles – use two or three
suspended above a rectangular kitchen table.

Let's get started!

I hope I have managed, with some of these ideas, to fire you with
enthusiasm to apply a fresh eye to what you already have, so that
by adding a little extra here and there you can create totally new
surroundings at home. It is not necessary to spend a fortune to
create a new environment for yourself and your family. It really
can be done very 'professionally' for a small outlay which you
can spread widely, as you develop your style. All you really need
is confidence married to a little careful thought and a pinch of
discipline, plus some time spent in your local library.

Don't forget to make up storyboards for each room using your
chosen colour and fabric scheme and to plan carefully so you are
totally happy with the scheme before you start work. Lastly, I
hope you have as much fun and gain as much creative stimulus as
I have done in preparing this book for you.

Curtains

The range of effects you can create with your style of curtaining is almost unlimited. Different colours, patterns, borders or curtain lengths can transform the looks and atmosphere of a room. And you don't have to be an expert at sewing to achieve a really stunning look in your home.

While you are planning what will best suit your room, here is a simple guide to some of the basic options you will need to consider.

Curtains

Think about the effects of a plain fabric, or a bold or delicate pattern in your room. Experiment with the length of the curtains. Do you want them just to touch the windowsill, fall slightly below it, hang full-length or drape on the floor?

Borders can create interesting effects, or you can add a frill, piping or a tasselled or fringed braid to the edges.

Lining

Lining the curtains gives them extra thickness and improves the way they hang. An interlining is an extra layer between curtain and lining. This gives an even fuller, more luxurious look as well as filtering out light and preserving heat in the room.

Heading tape

There are several different types of heading tape available. Standard heading tape is narrow and is positioned about 5cm (2in) below the top of the curtain to create a frill above soft gathers. The curtains need to be at least one and a half times the width of the window, so if your window is 2.4m (8ft) wide, you would need two 120cm (48in) widths for each curtain.

Pencil pleat heading tape is

positioned at the top of the curtain and gives a deeper, evenly gathered heading. The curtains need to be two and a half times the width of the window.

Triple pleat heading tape also gives a deep heading at the top of the curtain which falls in triple pleats. The curtains need to be two and a half times the width of the window.

Accessories

Think about whether you are hanging nets behind the curtains, and whether you are making valances, pelmets or tiebacks.

~ Café curtains ~

These frilled café curtains are ideal for many windows.

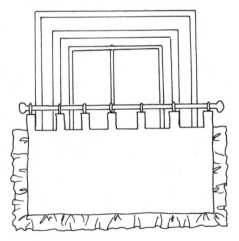

Fig. 1 **For a window which is not overlooked, a café curtain is a decorative alternative.**

You will need

1 Pole, width of window plus overhanging amount (10–12.5cm (4–5in) at each side for fixing.
2 Pole fixings and rings.
3 Fabric, the width of the pole by length to sill minus 5cm (2in) for frill. To this amount add 1.5cm (⅝in) all round for seam allowances.
4 Lining fabric, the same amount as main fabric.
5 Frill fabric, 8cm (3¼in) wide by twice the length of sides and bottom of curtain.
6 Pattern paper and piece of cardboard about 8cm (3¼in) square.
7 Pins.
8 Thread to match fabric.

To make pattern

1 On a large sheet of paper, draw out finished curtain shape without seam allowances.
2 Measure length of pole and add 2cm (¾in) for finished length. Divide length into 10cm (4in) sections, each section representing a loop and cut-out. You may have to adjust measurements to fit your pole. Now make template square from cardboard measuring 8cm (3¼in) square. Using template, draw in squares along top of curtain line with gaps of 2cm (¾in) between each square, starting and finishing with a gap.
3 Add seam allowances of 1.5cm (⅝in) (see Fig. 2) all round curtain shape on pattern.

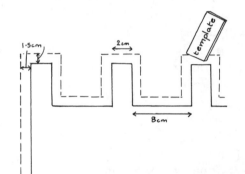

Fig. 2 **Add seam allowances of 1.5cm (⅝in) around top of pattern.**

To cut out

4 Lay fabric over lining, lay pattern on top, pin together and cut out.

To sew

5 Make up frill length, joining frill strips where necessary on straight grain with 1cm (⅜in) seam allowances pressed open. Fold in two lengthways, wrong sides together and press. Tuck in short ends of frill and slipstitch (see Sewing techniques) closed to neaten. Press, then stitch two lines of gathering stitches along seam allowance of 1.5cm (⅝in), breaking stitching half way. Pull up gently to equal the sides and bottom of curtain.

6 If you need to join fabric widths refer to Step 23 of Lined curtains on p. 50. Mark centre of frill length, then measure side of curtain from 8cm (3¼in) down to bottom corner. Double this length and mark in from each end of frill for corner points. Mark bottom centre point of curtain, then attach gathering evenly, right sides together, beginning and ending 8cm (3¼in) down from top raw edge of curtain, matching raw edges and marked centre point. Make sure gathers are even and there is enough frill fabric at corners for the frill to lie flat. Stitch all round.

7 Attach lining to curtain, right sides together and enclosing frill. Pin carefully around heading extensions, then stitch all round, leaving a gap of 25cm (10in) at bottom through which to turn. Trim diagonally across all heading points and clip into corners. Turn through to right side. Press carefully, then slipstitch (see Sewing techniques) closed bottom gap and press again.

8 Sew a ring to each heading extension and hang to finish.

~ Fringed curtain edges ~

There is a vast range of fringing or tasselled fringing to suit any curtains. Decide where you wish the fringing to lie: on leading edges of curtains the fringed heading will probably be stitched within 1cm (⅜in) of the edge.

You will need

1 Fringing twice the full length of curtain plus 5cm (2in) for neatening.
2 Pins.
3 Thread to match fringing.

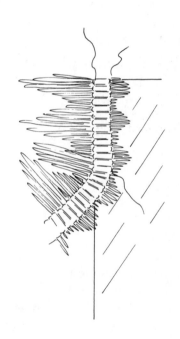

To sew

1 Pin carefully down inner leading edge from top to bottom, allowing an extra amount for neatening at top and bottom. Turn under raw top end of fringing and slipstitch (see Sewing techniques) to close. Slipstitch invisibly from top to bottom of fringing at both sides of heading, then neaten lower raw edge of fringing as before. See Fig. 1.

Fig. 1 **Attach scallop-shaped fringing to leading edges of curtains for instant 'oomph'.**

～ Narrow curtain binding ～

A narrow binding gives an attractive finish to a curtain edge. It is generally only used on the leading or inside edge of the curtain. Your fabric requirements will be the length of curtain plus 5cm (2in). This may seem wasteful, but joining binding strips will look ugly and remaining fabric can be used for matching tiebacks, further bindings or cushion covers (a standard floor-length curtain will provide six cushion covers).

You will need

1 Fabric strips for leading edges, 10cm (4in) wide for binding 2.5cm (1in) wide, twice finished length of curtain plus 2.5cm (1in) at each end for neatening.
2 Pins.
3 Thread to match binding.

To sew

1 Cut two leading edge bindings, joining where necessary on bias (see Sewing techniques).
2 On each long side of bindings, press under 2.5cm (1in) to wrong side. Attach one long edge to leading edge of curtain and pin, turning over 2.5cm (1in) at top and bottom of binding to neaten Stitch from top to bottom along pressed line.

3 Press binding away from curtain, then wrap over to wrong side and set folded binding edge in place flat against stitching line. See Fig. 1. Pin, then slipstitch (see Sewing techniques) into position from top to bottom, stitching across top and bottom to neaten. Press to finish.

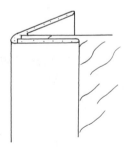

Fig. 1 **Binding wrapped to wrong side ready for slipstitching to finish.**

To decorate a window giving very little natural light, try a fixed, gathered curtain heading set on a pelmet or pole with a deep ruffle above the gathering. Drape curtains from a closed position at the heading to be tied back at windowsill length at each side of the sill, so they fall softly to break on the floor. You might also repeat the ruffling at inner leading edges of the curtains.

Where you can, treat curtains in the same way, adding borders to too-short curtains with a contrast fabric matching the room colours. You could also border the leading (inside) edges of the curtains, adding tiebacks to match.

～ Curtain borders ～

Wide borders can create a stunning effect, using contrasting or complementary fabrics, colours and patterns. For borders without joins, buy fabric the same measurement as the length and/or width of the curtain plus neatening allowances.

You will need

1 Fabric 30cm (12in) wide for leading edges, twice finished length of curtain plus 2.5cm (1in) at each end for neatening (see Step 1 of Narrow curtain binding on p. 42). At this stage you can decide if you would like extra length on curtains, so they drape on the floor.
2 Fabric 60cm (24in) wide for bottom borders, twice finished width of curtain plus 5cm (2in) at outer sides only for neatening. Leading edge border suggested here is 7.5cm (3in) wide and bottom border 15cm (6in) wide.
3 Pins and weights.
4 Thread to match borders.

To sew

1 Prepare two leading edge and two bottom strips of fabric, joining if necessary on the bias (see Sewing techniques for cutting and joining bias strips).

2 Unpick heading tape at top of leading edge of curtain for 10cm (4in).
3 Unpick hem of curtain fabric and lining, reserving any weights. Iron flat, using cloth and steam iron held 10cm (4in) away from fabric when ironing velvet. Laying the curtain hem flat, tack across the bottom foldline through lining. Trim curtain and lining 15cm (6in) below original foldline.
4 Take bottom edging strips and press 15cm (6in) to wrong side along each long edge.
5 Unfold pressed edging at one long side and set one end against front leading edge of curtain, right sides together, so lower pressed line matches original foldline of curtain. Tack along pressed line to outside edge, folding in seam allowance at the end. See Fig. 1.
6 Press border away from curtain and fold remaining long edge over bottom raw edge of curtain to stitching line on lining, forming a 15cm (6in) border. Pin, then

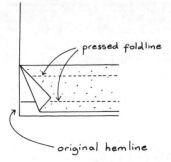

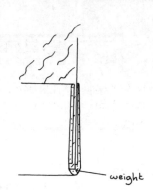

Fig. 1 Border set in position at lower raw edge of curtain.

Fig. 2 Finished border showing position of weight.

slipstitch along border (see Sewing techniques), inserting a weight with a few invisible hand stitches into each hem corner. Slipstitch closed outer border end to neaten. See Fig. 2.

7 Taking leading edge strips, press 7.5cm (3in) to wrong side along each long edge. Lay one opened out strip with its outer raw edge matching leading edge of curtain, right sides together, beginning at top by folding under 2.5cm (1in) to neaten. See Fig. 3. Pin, then stitch down length along outer pressed fold, neatening at bottom as at top.

8 Fold under remaining pressed edge and wrap border to wrong side so inner pressed edge touches stitching line. Slipstitch into place and across top and bottom of border to neaten.

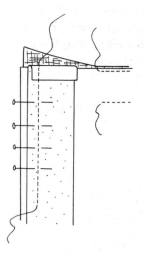

Fig. 3 Border set in position at leading edge of top of curtain.

9 Restitch heading tape into place and press completed borders carefully to finish.

Use curtaining as a room divider. Even more private than
a screen, curtains can be hung from the ceiling in loose
drapes to divide a dining room from a sitting area, for
example.

∼ Lined curtains ∼

These curtains are perfect for track or pole, and you can use whatever
heading tape you prefer. The instructions include an optional interlining.

You will need

1 Track or pole (see step 3)
   plus fixings.
2 Hooks or rings and hooks.
3 Weights.
4 Heading tape (see step 16).
5 Curtain fabric (see steps 13
   and 14).
6 Lining fabric (see steps 13
   and 14).
7 Interlining fabric (optional,
   see Interlining section).
8 Straight edge rule.
9 Set square (or large format
   sheets of newspaper).
10 Tailor's chalk.
11 Pins.
12 Thread to match curtain
   fabric and lining.

To make a plan

1 Decide length of curtain and if
drape is required onto floor (see
step 12).
2 Choose heading type and
depth. This can be 7.5cm (5in) or
15cm (6in). Depth required
generally depends on drop of
curtain – deeper headings
generally match longer lengths.
3 Decide on width of curtains
beyond window surround,
between 30 and 40cm (12–16in)
to give maximum light at the
window. This will give you the
length of track you need.
4 Draw a plan of your window,
marking in measurements
required. See Fig. 1.

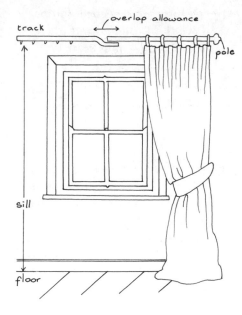

Fig. 1 Positions of pole and track with overlap allowance for track.

To calculate fabric requirements

width:

6 Measure length of pole or track and multiply by 2½ times (but check instructions for fullness given for manufacturer's tape as they do vary). To this amount add 5cm (2in) for each side hem. If the track has an overlap arm in the centre, add an allowance for the length of the overlap.

7 Divide total measurement by one fabric width, not including selvedge, and round this calculation up to nearest width. This should be sufficient to allow for joins in fabric widths which will require seam allowances of 1.5cm (⅝in) each side of the join.

8 Halve total arrived at in step 3 to get total number of widths required per curtain, positioning any half widths at outer edge of each curtain.

length:

9 Measure finished length planned for curtain, from top of track or further above it if you wish heading to be higher, or from just under pole, to windowsill, floor or drape onto floor.

To fix pole or track

5 Following manufacturer's instructions, fix pole or track into position above window, either in window recess or extended beyond each side of window to give more light or the impression of a larger window. The height of pole or track above window is usually set between 7.5cm (3in) and 12cm (5in).

10 Now add heading tape depth plus 3cm (1¼in) for top seam allowance to length.

11 Add depth of one fold-back for hem, from 10cm (4in) to 15cm (6in) depending on length of curtains. A curtain less than 1m (3ft 3in) long only requires the minimum hem. A full-length curtain needs the maximum.

12 For floor-length curtains which drape onto floor, add amount of drape required, between 7.5cm (3in) and 10cm (4in), to the overall length.

total fabric requirements:
13 Multiply total length needed by number of widths to get fabric requirement.

14 Lastly, fabric allowance must be made for any pattern repeat, which is matched across seams and the pair of curtains when closed. Simply add one pattern repeat (its length will be marked on the selvedge, or measure from beginning of one section to beginning of next identical section) per width of fabric required, after first width. You now have the total main fabric requirements.

15 Lining fabric requirement will be total arrived at in step 13 less 8cm (3¼in) per width, providing fabric is same width.

16 Heading tape needed will be total width of each curtain, less hems and seams, plus seam allowances at each side of 5cm (2in) plus an extra 15cm (6in) for adjustment.

To cut out

17 The most important part of curtain making is to get curtains square, and to press carefully at each stage of the making-up process. Start at the bottom of the fabric pattern. Use a set square or newspaper and pins to achieve an even hem, lining up one corner of set square or paper with edge of fabric selvedge. Draw a straight line on the right side of fabric across the width or 'weft' of fabric where a row of design repeats begins and mark it with chalk. This will form the hemline. Measure length of curtain line inclusive of top turning allowance and mark across with chalk. Add hem allowance at bottom of curtain length and mark across with chalk.

18 Cut out curtain width and mark top with two notches cut into turning allowance.

19 Find next row of pattern repeats, mark across, then measure and cut curtain width as

Example

width:

Pole length 2m (6ft 6in) × 2½ (2)	5.00m	(196¼in)
Side hems (2)	20cm	(8in)
Overlap (2)	20cm	(8in)
	5.40m	(212in)
Divided by one fabric width (3)	1.20m	(47in)
Actual fabric widths (3)	4.50m	(176⅝in)
Rounded up to 5 fabric widths (3)		
Allowance for 4 joins (12cm/4¾in) available within calculations (3)		

length:

Finished length (5)	3.50m	(137⅜in)
Heading tape depth (6)	30cm	(11¾in)
Top seam allowance (6)	30cm	(11¾in)
Hem (7)	15cm	(6in)
Drape (8)	10cm	(4in)
	4.35m	(170¾in)

totals:

Multiply curtain length by number of widths (9)	4.35m 5	(170¾in)
	21.75m	(853¾in)
Add pattern repeat 30cm (11¾in) × 4 widths	1.20m	(47in)
	22.95m	(900¾in)
Lining (11)	21.75m	(853¾in)
Less 8cm (3¼in) × 5 widths	40cm	(15⅝in)
	21.35m	(838in)
Heading tape 5 widths × 120cm (47in)	6.00m	(235½in)
Less side hems and joins	32cm	(12⅝in)
Plus side hems and adjustment	35cm	(13¾in)
	6.03m	(236¾in)

before. Trim away any excess fabric below hem allowance.

20 Repeat until all lengths have been cut, then cut any half-widths by folding fabric in half lengthways, lining up selvedges and cutting carefully up fold to measured top of each length.

21 Cut off all selvedges and press all lengths of fabric.

22 Repeat steps 1 to 5 for lining, shortening each length by 8cm (3¼in).

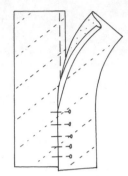

Fig. 2 **Pressed seam allowance set in position to match pattern.**

To sew

23 Match print by pressing under a seam allowance of one length and placing it against the unpressed edge of another length's seam allowance so that pattern matches. Ladderstitch across join (see Sewing techniques), then fold fabric right sides together and stitch. See Fig. 2. Press seam allowances open. Repeat for remaining lengths to form a pair of curtains, positioning any half-widths at outer edges.

24 Repeat for lining, omitting print matching instructions.

When making curtains, use fabric at least two and a half times the width of track or pole. If the expense is excessive, choose a cheaper fabric and use your expensive one where it will show to greater effect, in cushions for example. Remember that more, cheaper fabric is always preferable to less, expensive cloth, which will look mean if not used luxuriously. For the best results, use inexpensive fabric interlined to make it look heavier and plumper.

25 Press 5cm (2in) to wrong side down each side of curtain.

26 Turn up hem allowance and press, folding mitred corners (see Sewing techniques). Stitch curtain weights into each corner and slipstitch (see Sewing techniques) closed. Stitch further weights at each fabric join if required, then slipstitch edges of mitres together.

27 Herringbone stitch (see Sewing techniques) down each side and along hem of curtain. If you are going to interline the curtains, refer to the Interlining section at the end of the project before continuing.

28 Lay curtain flat, wrong side uppermost to mark in chalk lines down the curtain where you will lockstitch curtain to lining. Using a metre stick, mark down centre of curtain from top to just above hem edge. Mark further vertical lines across the curtain, about 30cm (12in) apart.

29 Set wrong side of lining on top of curtain at its centre, matching top edges, then pin down length of lining and curtain and fold lining back against pins. Lockstitch (see Sewing techniques) lining to curtain fabric, beginning 10cm (4in) from top and ending 2.5cm (1in) from hem.

30 Repeat pinning procedure at next chalkline and lockstitch, working outwards both ways until lining is attached.

31 Trim lining at each side of curtain so it matches folded edge of curtain. Fold 2cm (¾in) of trimmed lining edge to wrong side and press. Fold hem lining edge 4cm (1½in) to wrong side and press. Slipstitch (see Sewing techniques) pressed folded edges of lining to folded in curtain, thus leaving a 2cm (¾in) margin around sides and hem of curtain. Tack lining and curtain together at top raw edges.

32 Turn down top of curtain to lining side by heading depth and pin.

33 To attach heading tape, cut tape to curtain width plus 10cm (4in), checking you have matching pleat positions at inner edges of curtains. At inner edges of tapes, free cords for 4cm (1½in) and knot. Trim tape to within 6mm (¼in) of knots. Turn under 1.5cm (⅝in) so knots fall at back and will be sewn behind the tape. At outer edges of tapes, free cords for 6.5cm (2½in) but do not knot. Trim tape to within 12mm (½in) of cords and turn under 6mm (¼in).

34 Set outer edge of tape with loose cords against outer edge of curtain back, 3mm (⅛in) down from folded top edge. Pin, then attach and pin tape across width of curtain. Stitch along top and bottom of tape, from side to side of curtain, stitching each line in same direction to avoid pulling.

35 Pull up cords of heading tape to correct width of curtain. Do not cut but knot together neatly; cords will have to be released when curtains are cleaned. Thread hooks through tape at even intervals, positioning a hook at either end and checking height of heading formed against track, making sure it is concealed behind heading. Hang to finish.

Interlining

Interlining valances and curtains will give a much fuller, more luxurious look as well as filtering out any light when drawn and preserving heat in the room. Fix the interlining before lining the curtains (after step 27).

1 You will need the same amount of interlining as lining.

2 Cut lengths as for lining. Join interlining lengths by overlapping the long edges by 1.5cm (⅝in) and using a herringbone stitch (see Sewing techniques) to join together.

3 Mark lockstitch lines (steps 6 and 7) onto curtain fabric and interlining. Lay interlining down onto wrong side of curtain or valance, matching top edges, side turnings and hemline. Lockstitch into position.

4 Continue with lining attachment (step 6).

Sewing frilling down the leading inner edges of curtains and around their hems can soften an otherwise austere fabric. You could try using contrast piping between the main fabric and frill, then making shaped tiebacks with the same contrast piping and frilling around top and bottom of tieback or bottom only for a matching effect.

Valances

You can utilise the space above your window both decoratively – creating interesting and different looks with a pelmet or valance – and to make the most of space. You can opt for a straight valance, or those who are more experienced might like to experiment with a shaped valance, or add fringing or narrow borders to match the curtains.

~ Shaped valance ~

This shaped valance is emphasised by a narrow border. It is lined and interlined to give a full effect and hung on a valance pelmet. Curtains can be added in the same print and edged with a matching contrast border. Matching tiebacks will complete the picture.

You will need

1 Main fabric (see step 4).
2 Lining fabric (see step 5).
3 Optional stiff interlining (see step 6).
4 Contrast bias fabric for border (see step 7).
5 Manufacturer's heading tape, 7.5cm (3in) deep, length of pattern (see step 2) plus extra 5cm (2in) at each end and 15cm (6in) for adjustment.
6 Curtain hooks.
7 Cardboard, 50cm (19⅝in) deep by half length of track.
8 Long sheets of pattern paper or decorator's lining paper at least 70cm (27⅝in) wide.
9 Tailor's chalk.
10 Pins.
11 Thread to match fabric and lining.

For an attractive treatment try adding a border to a fixed shaped valance and the leading edges of matching curtains.

To make pattern

1 Make a cardboard template half length of track and depth of planned valance at outside point, here 50cm (19⅝in). The valance should be about one-sixth of the length of the curtains. Mark template vertically into three equal sections, A at outide, B in middle and C nearest centre of pelmet track. Mark in deepest point of valance, 50cm (19⅝in) from top, at outside edge of A. Mark 38cm (15in) drops at remaining joins of template sections. See Fig. 1. Beginning at outside edge of A, draw a curved, then straight line marking lower edge of valance, to inner edge of C. Cut round outside edge of template and attach to one half of pelmet with sticky tape, setting top of template 2.5cm (1in) above top edge of pelmet and wrapping around pelmet returns. Check shape and depth of valance, adjust where necessary and remove. Cut template into sections A, B and C.

2 Join a strip of pattern paper to achieve length of track multiplied by 2½, plus seam allowances at each end of 5cm (2in). Fold in half lengthways, then mark into three equal sections vertically, marked A, B and C, starting with A at the outside edge. Draw a line

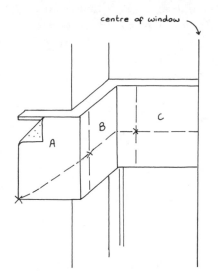

Fig. 1 **Half-sketch showing the position of shaped valance on pelmet board.**

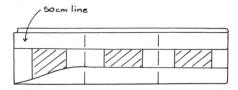

Fig. 2 **Folded pattern paper showing position of template within each equal section.**

50cm (19⅝in) up from bottom of paper pattern. Place top of template against drawn line in centre of paper section A. Place template B against centre of B, and template C against centre of C. See Fig. 2. Draw in finished bottom shape of valance as shown, following template markers.

3 To 50cm (19⅝in) line add 7.5cm (3in) for top turning allowance. Cut out pattern.

To calculate fabric requirements

4 Main fabric will have to be joined to achieve width of pattern. Measure how many widths fit into pattern, not including selvedges, and rounding up to nearest width. Allow 5cm (2in) for side hems, plus 1.5cm (⅝in) for seams on each side of each width for joining. Multiply the number of widths by the total depth required at deepest point of valance. If matching prints, measure pattern repeat and add one pattern repeat per width, after first width, for total fabric requirements. (For a valance which is not interlined, add two fabric widths at centre for extra fullness.)

5 Lining fabric requirement will be the same as main fabric, omitting extra for pattern matching.

6 Interlining should be width of valance (see pattern), 15cm (6in) deep.

7 Contrast bias cut border fabric will be total length of main fabric required for valance (see pattern) plus extra 2.5cm (1in) for neatening at outside edges. Cut the border fabric 30cm (12in) wide for a 7.5cm (3in) border. 100cm (39¼in) of 122cm (48in) wide fabric will give you 296cm (116¼in) of bias border strip.

Example

Pattern width	5.50m	(215¾in)
Side hems	5cm	(2in)
	5.55m	(217¾in)
Divided by one fabric width	1.20m	(47in)
Actual fabric widths	4.62m	(178⅜in)
Rounded up to 6 fabric widths		
Allowance for 5 joins (12cm/4¾in) available within calculations		
Depth of valance	57.5cm	(22⅝in)
Multiply valance depth by number of widths for fabric and lining requirement	6	
	3.45m	(135½in)
Add pattern repeat 15cm (6in) × 5 widths	75cm	(29½in)
	4.20m	(165in)
Interlining 5.50m × 15cm (215¾in × 6in)		
Bias fabric 2.50m × 122cm (108⅛in × 47⅞in) wide fabric	2.50m	(98⅖in)

To cut out

8 Cut out widths required, beginning by drawing a line across start of pattern repeat and measuring total length required below it. Cut across fabric, then find next pattern repeat and continue until all widths are cut. Remove selvedges.

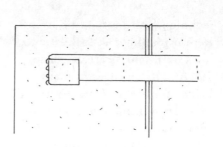

Fig. 3 **Position of optional interlining at valance head.**

To sew

9 Attach valance widths by firstly matching patterns. Press one side of seam allowance at each fabric width join to wrong side. Set over next width to be joined until pattern is matched. Pin, then ladderstitch (see Sewing techniques) seam. Fold fabric right sides together and stitch down seamline. Repeat for other joins and press seam allowances open. Repeat for lining, omitting matching instructions.

10 If heading tape is not stiff, stiffen wrong side of valance heading by attaching interlining 7.5cm (3in) down from top raw edges. Lockstitch (see Sewing techniques) every 30cm (12in) from top to bottom along complete valance length, following instructions given in step 11. If applying full interlining, lay interlining down onto wrong side of fabric, matching top edges, valance side turnings and hemline. Lockstitch into position following the instructions given below. See Fig. 3.

11 Set main fabric over lining fabric, wrong sides together, enclosing interlining and matching inner seamlines and raw edges. Pin at top and bottom, then lay paper pattern over fabrics, matching top edges. Mark off bottom curve of valance with chalk or pins and cut. Remove lining. Starting with a centre line, mark in vertical chalklines down wrong side of fabric, 30cm (12in) apart. Mark central vertical line on lining. Set wrong sides of lining and fabric together, matching raw edges and central lines. Pin down central line, then fold lining back against pins and lockstitch (see Sewing techniques) from top to bottom. Repeat pinning and lockstitching lines until fabrics are attached.

12 At outside edges of main fabric, press 5cm (2in) to wrong side. Trim lining fabric at each edge so it matches folded main fabric edge, then fold lining 2cm (¾in) to wrong side and press. Slipstitch (see Sewing techniques) pressed edges of lining to folded in valance, leaving a 2cm (¾in) margin at each side. Neaten top raw edges of valance together.

13 Prepare border strip, joining on bias where necessary (see Sewing techniques). Press 7.5cm (3in) to wrong side along each long edge. Open out one foldline and lay along lower edge of valance, right sides together and matching raw edges, folding under 2.5cm (1in) at each end to neaten. Pin, then stitch along foldline. Press border away from valance, wrap over to wrong side and set folded pressed edge to stitch line. Slipstitch (see Sewing techniques) from side to side and across neatened ends to finish. Press.

14 Turn down top of valance to lining side by heading depth of 7.5cm (3in) and pin. Cut heading tape to width of valance plus 10cm (4in), matching outer pleats at each end. Free cords at one end for 4cm (1½in) and knot. Trim tape to within 6mm (¼in) of knots. Turn under 1.5cm (⅝in) so knots fall at back and will be enclosed by stitching. At other end of tape, free cords for 6.5cm (2½in) but do not knot. Trim tape to within 12mm (½in) of cords and turn under 6mm (¼in).

15 Set tape against valance back, 3mm (⅛in) down from folded top edge. Pin tape across width of valance. Stitch along top and bottom of tape from side to side, stitching each line in the same direction to avoid pulling.

16 Pull up cords of tape to correct width of valance. Do not cut, but knot neatly together, since cords will have to be released when valance is cleaned. Thread hooks through tape at regular intervals, positioning a hook at each end and checking height of heading formed will lie 1cm (⅜in) above top of pelmet. Place outside edges of valance around returns of pelmet to conceal it. Readjust hooks in tape to match the position of the eyelet rings in pelmet shelf (see step 6, Pelmet shelf on p. 62) if necessary. Then hang the completed valance, beginning by hooking each outside edge through an eyelet ring around returns of pelmet shelf. Attach central hook to central ring and continue hooking each hook through its matching ring to finish.

～ Gathered and bound ～ ～ valance ～

For those with a pole rather than a pelmet fixing, this simple bordered valance will make a real difference to your window.

You will need

1 Pole, width of window plus overlaps, 12.5cm (5in) in diameter.
2 Main fabric (see steps 1 and 2).
3 Lining fabric (see step 3).
4 Contrast bias fabric for binding top and bottom of valance (see step 4).
5 Pins.
6 Thread to match fabric and lining.

To calculate fabric requirements

1 Fabric will have to be joined to achieve width, so measure pole and multiply by 2½ times. Add 2.5cm (1in) for hems at outside edges. Divide this amount by width of fabric minus selvedges and round up to nearest width. This should allow for 1.5cm (⅝in) on each side of each width for joining.

2 Decide depth of valance below pole, here 38cm (15in). The valance should be about one-sixth of the length of the curtains. Add pole channel allowance of 7.5cm (3in) plus 8cm (3¼in) for top frill. Multiply this measurement by number of widths needed. If matching prints, measure pattern repeat and add one pattern repeat measurement for each width after first one for total fabric requirements.

Example

Pole length 2m (6ft 6in) × 2½	5.00m	(196¼in)
Side hems	5cm	(2in)
	5.05m	(198¼in)
Divided by one fabric width	1.20m	(47¼in)
Actual fabric widths	4.20m	(165in)
Rounded up to 5 fabric widths		
Allowance for 4 joins (12cm/4¾in) available within calculations		
Depth of valance below pole	38cm	(15in)
Pole channel allowance	7.5cm	(3in)
Top frill	8cm	(3¼in)
	53.5cm	(21in)
Multiply valance length	53.5cm	(21in)
by number of widths for fabric and lining requirement	5	
	2.675m	(105in)
Add pattern repeat 15cm (6in) × 4 widths	60cm	(23⅝in)
	3.275m	(128½in)
Bias fabric: 5 widths plus 4 × 10cm (4in) joins		

3 Lining fabric requirement will be the same as main fabric, omitting extra for pattern matching.

4 Contrast bias fabric for binding will be twice total width of valance plus 10cm (4in) extra for each bias join and 2.5cm (1in) for outside neatened edges at end of both strips. Cut bias 10cm (4in) wide for 2.5cm (1in) finished binding width.

To cut out

5 Cut out main and lining fabric widths required, drawing a line across main fabric width at beginning of print repeat and measuring down total length required. Cut across, then draw another line across width at beginning of next repeat and continue until all widths have been cut.

To sew

6 Attach valance widths by firstly matching prints. Press one side of seam allowance at each fabric width join to wrong side. Set over next width to be joined until pattern is matched. Pin, then ladderstitch (see Sewing techniques) seam. Fold fabric right sides together and stitch down seamline. Repeat for other joins and press seam allowances open. Repeat for lining, omitting matching instructions.

7 Set main fabric over lining fabric, wrong sides together, matching seamlines and raw edges. Pin, then tack at top and bottom. Press under 2.5cm (1in) at each end of main and lining fabric to inside and tack.

8 Make two binding strips by joining contrast strips on bias (see Sewing techniques). Each one should be full width of valance plus neatening allowances of 2.5cm (1in) at each end. Press seam allowances open, then press 2.5cm (1in) to wrong side along one long edge of each binding strip.

9 Lay unpressed edge of one binding strip right sides together and matching raw edges, along top of valance, folding in 2.5cm (1in) at each short end to neaten. Pin, then stitch along 2.5cm (1in) seamline from side to side. Press binding away from valance, then wrap over to wrong side and set folded pressed edge to stitchline. Slipstitch (see Sewing techniques) from side to side and across neatened ends to finish. Repeat for lower edge of valance and press.

10 To form channel for pole, measure 8cm (3¼in) down from top edge of valance and mark a pinline along complete width. Mark a further pinline 7.5cm (3in) down from first line. Stitch along each pinline, beginning at same side for each stitching line to avoid pulling. Slipstitch (see Sewing techniques) closed sideseams of valance at each side of channel and remove tacking. See Fig. 1. Insert pole into valance channel, adjusting gathers evenly to finish.

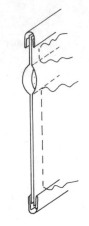

Fig. 1 **Cross-section of gathered and bound valance showing position of bindings and channel.**

～ Pelmet shelf ～

A simple shelf fixed above a bay window provides the base for attaching a valance.

You will need

1 Wooden planking, plywood or hardboard, 9cm (3½in) wide by 2cm (¾in) deep.
2 Four fixing plates (7.5cm/ 3in).
3 Ten angle brackets (7.5cm/ 3in).
4 Eyelet rings for fixing valance.
5 Drill.
6 Plastic wallplugs.
7 Screws for plates and brackets to match.
8 Screwdriver.
9 Book.

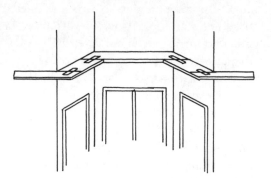

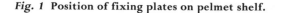

Fig. 1 **Position of fixing plates on pelmet shelf.**

To make

1 See Fig. 1. Measure wall above curtain track from corner to corner of central bay. Set book in corner of central bay, mark off 9cm (3½in) width of pelmet on book, then measure extra amount required on outer edge of planking to reach angled side of bay. Repeat for other corner and cut length of planking to these measurements.

2 Measure wall from inner to outer edge of side bay and place a further wooden plank of at least this measurement along side bay, beginning at inner corner. Mark off outside corner of side bay, then mark a line on the plank which continues the line of the outside flat wall. Remove and place against central bay plank on floor, so it underlaps central bay plank and inner bay corners touch. Mark off angle of central plank on side plank and trim along marked line. Repeat for other angled bay side plank. Trim outer lines on side bay planking.

3 Set another plank along angle cut, matching inner corners, so that the plank extends 40cm (15⅝in) along the flat wall. Mark angled inner bay line along edge of plank, then trim along line.

4 Set fixing plates at each plank join, marking position of screws.

Select drill bit one size smaller than screw size, drill holes and screw planks together to form finished pelmet shape. See Fig. 1.

5 To fix pelmet, set in position at required height above track and mark positions of angle bracket screw holes, placing one bracket to just within each side of each plank piece. Remove pelmet and attach brackets to wall, drilling holes, inserting wallplugs and screwing brackets into place.

6 Now set pelmet in position and mark positions of bracket screws. Remove, drill holes in pelmet and reset in position, screwing into place on wall. If you wish, paint pelmet to match wall colouring. Screw eyelet rings into pelmet along narrow outside edge, placing one at each end of outside edges of pelmet where they touch wall and at outer corners, then spacing 5cm (2in) apart to finish.

No time to make a valance? Then simply line a length of fabric with contrast fabric to match the curtains and wrap luxuriously around a curtain pole so tails hang down each side. Interline it if you can for a richer look, edging the lower long edge with fringing or contrast binding, for example, and making tiebacks to match. Experiment with a sheet folded double lengthways to find the length required (one width of fabric should be enough) and don't be afraid to experiment with different ways of wrapping the pole – with the tail hanging down on one side only, for example. The results can be much more stunning than ordinary valances and cheaper and quicker to achieve.

Tiebacks

Tiebacks are simple to make but give a really professional finish to your curtains. Fix a small cup hook to the wall at the appropriate height at each curtain edge to hook on the tiebacks.

~ Bow tiebacks ~

These simple tiebacks add a charming feminine touch to the decor.

You will need

1 Fabric, 26cm (10¼in) of 122cm (48in) wide for two tiebacks, 10cm (4in) wide, when finished.
2 Contrast fabric for binding/lining to make four strips 19cm (7½in) wide by 122cm (48in) long. You will need 122cm (48in) of fabric of the same width.
3 Two small rings.
4 Pins.
5 Thread to match fabric.

To sew

1 Cut out strips of fabric and contrast following the measurements given here. Set one fabric strip against one contrast lining strip, right sides together and matching raw edges. Pin and stitch along each long edge of fabric and lining strip from end to end. Press seam allowances away from main fabric, turn and press flat so that a strip of contrast fabric 1.5cm (⅝in) wide creates a binding down each long edge.
2 Draw a matching diagonal line across each raw end and cut, then turn under 1.5cm (⅝in) and slipstitch (see Sewing techniques) closed to neaten, trimming away excess seam allowances if necessary to flatten. See Fig. 1.

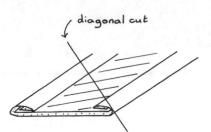

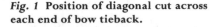

Fig. 1 **Position of diagonal cut across each end of bow tieback.**

3 Fold tie in half lengthways and sew a small ring to centre of fold's contrast side. Repeat for other tie and press to finish.
4 Hang the tiebacks on the wall hook and tie into a bow around the curtain.

Raid the remnant boxes of department stores for tapestry effect bits for cushion covers and tiebacks, edging them by hand with contrast bought braid. And don't forget that you can back them with simple lining fabric to save cost.

∼ Piped-edge tiebacks ∼

These classic tiebacks will add a luxurious touch to any room.

You will need

1 50cm (20in) of 135cm (54in) wide fabric.
2 Lining fabric as above.
3 Interlining as above.
4 Buckram or similar stiffening, as above.
5 Contrast bias cut piping fabric, length of outside edge of pattern plus 2.5cm (1in) for neatening. Cut width of measurement around piping plus 2.5cm (1in) for seam allowances plus allowance for bias joins.
6 Preshrunk piping cord, length of outside edge of pattern plus 2.5cm (1in).
7 Four small rings.
8 Pattern paper.
9 Pins.
10 Thread to match fabric.

To make pattern

1 Make a pattern of the curved shape. Fold pattern paper in half lengthways. Mark down fold 10cm (4in) from top, and down a further 12cm (4¾in). Mark a point 46cm (18in) along the top of folded paper. Beginning at first mark down fold, draw a line starting at right angles to fold and continuing up in a gentle curve to 46cm (18in) mark at paper top. Mark in another line beginning at lower fold point, starting at right angles and continuing at same spacing to first line, but narrowing towards top. Curve line from just before top point around top of tieback so width at top is 9cm (3⅝in), using mug or glass base for top curve if necessary. See Fig. 1.

2 Cut out pattern, which includes seam allowances of 1cm (⅜in).

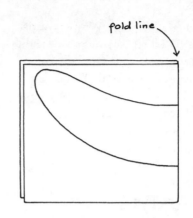

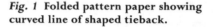

Fig. 1 **Folded pattern paper showing curved line of shaped tieback.**

To sew

3 Unfold pattern and cut out fabric, lining, interlining and buckram. Attach interlining to wrong side of fabric, matching raw edges, and tack into position. Trim buckram by 1cm (⅜in) all round and attach to wrong side of fabric and interlining, setting in 1cm (⅜in) all round from raw edges of fabric and interlining. Tack.

4 Cut and join contrast bias piping strips (see Sewing techniques). Measure seamline all round tieback, add 2.5cm (1in) joining allowance and cut piping cord to this measurement. Unravel a small section at each end of cord and overlap by joining allowance. Cut each strand at a different length and intertwine cut cords, whipping joined lengths together with thread and stitching to secure (see Circular piped cushion, Figs. 3

and 4 on p. 73). Wrap contrast piping fabric around cord, right side outside and tack all round, close to cord edge. To neaten, fold under one raw edge on bias and wrap over remaining raw edge of fabric (see Figs. 5 and 6, Circular piped cushion on p. 73). Slipstitch (see Sewing techniques) to close.

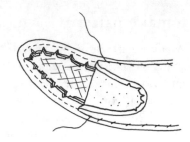

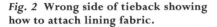

Fig. 2 **Wrong side of tieback showing how to attach lining fabric.**

5 Tack piping to right side of fabric, matching raw edges, and stitch all round using zip foot, clipping seam allowances around curves to ease. Fold all seam allowances to wrong side and tack. Set lining wrong sides together against tieback and pin into position, overlapping folded in edges by seam allowance. Fold in 1cm (⅜in) on lining edge and slipstitch (see Sewing techniques) all round. See Fig. 2.

6 Press completed tieback, then attach a small ring with handstitches to top back of each narrowed edge to finish.

Make plaited tiebacks with interlined 'tubes' of fabric in three closely related colours to match those in the room. Try cutting strips 7.5cm (3in) wide by the required length. They need to be long enough to go around the curtain beginning and finishing at the tieback hook. Attach interlining to the wrong side of each strip – you will need two of each colour for a set of curtains – and tack into place. Fold each strip in half lengthways, right sides together and stitch from end to end, stitching across ends and leaving a gap halfway along the long stitching line through which to turn the tieback inside out. Turn each tube the right way out, slipstitch closed and plait one of each colour together. Slipstitch three ends together at each end of the tieback and attach a small brass ring at each end to finish.

Cushions

~ Square frilled cushion ~

This cushion has a double raised frill and a displaced zip opening.

You will need

1 Cushion pad.
2 Zip, the length of one side of cushion, less 10cm (4in).
3 Main fabric, twice the measurements of cushion pad plus 1.5cm (⅝in) all round, plus 3cm (1¼in) extra on one edge of back cushion piece for zip seam allowances. Allow extra fabric for large prints, the width of pattern repeat.
4 Main frill fabric, 21cm (8⅜in) wide, 2½ times outside edges of pad plus 1.5cm (⅝in) joining allowances each end.
5 Contrast narrower frill fabric, 13cm (5⅛in) wide by 2½ times outside edges of pad, plus 15cm (⅝in) joining allowances each end.
6 Pattern paper.
7 Pins.
8 Thread to match fabric.

Example

44cm (17⅜in) of 135/138cm (53/54in) wide fabric will make three cushion covers.
44cm (17⅜in) of 122cm (48in) wide fabric will make two cushion covers.
Main frill will take 42cm (16½in) of either width fabric.
Contrast frill will take 26cm (10¼in) of either width fabric.
Allow extra fabric for large prints, up to one pattern repeat.

To make pattern

1 Cut two identical pattern pieces to measurements of pad plus 1.5cm (⅝in) all round. Mark one pattern 'front' and set aside. Draw a line through remaining

pattern marked 'back', 6.5cm
(2½in) down from one side. Cut
along this line and mark each cut
'add 1.5cm (⅝in)' for zip
opening. See Fig. 1.

To cut out

2 Set patterns on fabric,
following straight grain, allowing
for print design and zip
allowances and cut out. Cut frill
strips on straight grain.

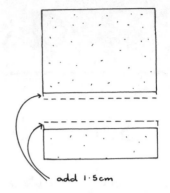

Fig. 1 **Adding zip seam allowances to back pattern.**

To sew

3 For back cushion, pin two back
pieces right sides together and
matching raw edges at zip
opening. Stitch for 5cm (2in) in
from each end. Tack remaining
opening closed, press seam
allowance open and insert zip (see
Sewing techniques).
4 Make main and contrast frills
by firstly joining frill strips into
required lengths with 1cm (⅜in)
seam allowances pressed open.
Fold main frill right sides
together lengthways, matching
raw edges, and stitch a 1.5cm
(⅝in) seamline. Turn channel
formed to right side using blunt
end of pencil, fold under

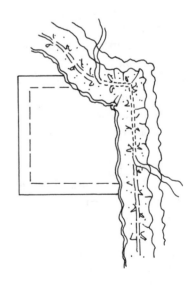

Fig. 2 **How to attach the double frill.**

1.5cm (⅝in) at one short end of channel and insert remaining short end into it for 1.5cm (⅝in) to form circle. Slipstitch to close. Roll seam allowance 1.5cm (⅝in) to wrong side and press flat all round circle. Repeat for contrast frill.

5 Mark main frill into four equal sections with pins. Set contrast frill against main frill with seamlines touching and inner folded edges matching. Pin together. Stitch two lines of gathering all round frills, 6mm (¼in) apart and beginning 1.5cm (⅝in) in from inner edge, breaking stitching lines at pin markers. Gather up each section to match a cushion side.

6 Mark chalk line all round front cushion piece, 6.5cm (2½in) from raw edges. Attach gathered double frill to front cushion with contrast frill next to right side of front, matching pins to corners, adjusting gathers and matching inner frills to chalk line. Pin, then stitch all round, following each line of gathering. Remove gathering stitches. See Fig. 2.

7 Open zip. Pin front to back cushion all round, right sides together, folding frill out of way. Stitch, trim corners and turn. Insert pad to finish.

Haunt jumble sales and second-hand shops for worn rugs to cut up and make into cushion covers which can be backed with plain lining fabric. Handsew the edges with braid to finish. Old bits of velvet also make beautiful cushions, backed in contrast fabric, or buy inexpensive white cotton velvet for elegantly plain sitting-room cushions.

～ Circular piped cushion ～

This circular cushion can have a piped or piped and bound frill. It also has the zip opening on the back of the cushion.

You will need

1 Cushion pad.
2 Main fabric twice measurements of cushion pad plus 1.5cm (⅝in) seam allowance all round, plus an extra 3cm (1¼in) to depth of fabric for zip seam allowances in back cushion piece. Allow extra fabric for large prints.
3 Contrast bias cut fabric for piping, length of circumference of cushion plus 1.5cm (⅝in) joining allowances, cut measurement around piping plus 3cm (1¼in) seam allowances. Bias strips cut 4cm (1⅝in) wide and joined where necessary will require: 518cm (203¼in) for 25cm (10in) of 122cm (48in) fabric; 1036cm (406½in) for 50cm (19⅝in) of the same width fabric; and 2072cm (813in) for 100cm (39¼in) of same.
4 Main fabric for frill 6.5cm (2⅝in) deep: 8cm (3¼in) wide by 2½ times circumference measurement plus 1.5cm (⅝in) joining allowances.
5 Contrast fabric for frill binding, 11cm (4⅜in) wide by 2½ times circumference measurement plus 1.5cm (⅝in) joining allowances.
6 Pattern paper.
7 Zip, length of line drawn one-third down paper pattern less 10cm (4in).
8 Pencil with length of string attached.
9 Piping cord, preshrunk, the length of circumference plus 5cm (2in) joining allowance.
10 Pins.
11 Thread to match fabric.

To make pattern

1 Measure across cushion pad at its widest point and add 3cm (1¼in). Fold one pattern paper in quarters, pin string at point half length of pad fabric measurement and pin into folded point of

paper. Draw an arc from side to side. Cut round marked line, unfold pattern and mark 'front'. See Fig. 1.

2 Copy pattern onto second paper piece. Draw line one-third down pattern and cut through, marking each piece 'back'. Mark each straight edge 'add 1.5cm (⅝in), for zip seam allowance'. See Fig. 2.

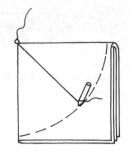

Fig. 1 **Making a circular pattern.**

To cut out

3 Set pattern pieces onto fabric, allowing for print positions and zip allowances, pin and cut out. Cut contrast piping on bias (see Sewing techniques) and main and contrast frill on straight grain of fabric.

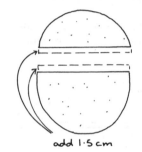

add 1.5 cm

Fig. 2 **Adding zip seam allowances to back pattern.**

To sew

4 Pin back pattern pieces right sides together and matching raw edges at zip opening. Stitch for 6.5cm (2½in) in from each end. Tack remaining opening closed, press seam allowances open and insert zip (see Sewing techniques).

5 Join bias fabric piping strips (see Sewing techniques). Unravel a small section at each end of piping cord, cutting each strand to a different length. Intertwine cut strands, checking circumference measurement, and whip joined lengths together with thread, stitching to secure. See Figs. 3 and 4. Wrap contrast piping fabric around cord, right side outside and raw edges matching. Tack all round, close to cord edge. To neaten, fold under one raw edge on bias and

Fig. 3 **Cut each piping cord strand to a different length.**

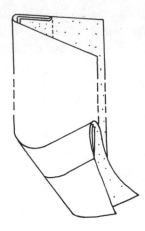

Fig. 7 **Match raw edges to form contrast binding for frill.**

Fig. 4 **Piping cord strands whipped together and stitched to secure.**

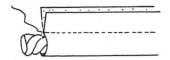

Fig. 5 **Stitch line set close as possible to piping cord.**

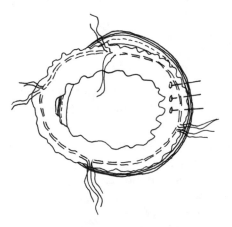

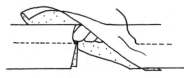

Fig. 6 **Bias-wrap starting point of piping and stitch to finish.**

Fig. 8 **Attaching frill to front cushion piece, sandwiching piping.**

wrap over remaining raw edge of fabric. See Figs. 5 and 6. Slipstitch (see Sewing techniques) to close.

6 Pin, then tack piping to front cushion piece, right sides together with raw edges even. Clip seam allowance of piping all round curves to ease. Stitch all round close to cord edge, using zip foot.

7 If attaching frill, firstly join main frill fabric where necessary on straight grain with 1cm (⅜in) seam allowances pressed open. Join contrast frill binding fabric as above, then join main frill strip to contrast binding strip along one long edge and stitch, taking 1.5cm (⅝in) seam allowance. Press contrast and seam allowances away from main fabric and stitch two ends right sides together to form a circle. Fold in half lengthways, wrong sides together and matching raw edges to form a contrast binding to folded frill edge. See Fig. 7. Pin, then divide into four even sections by folding in half twice and cutting a small notch in folds. Sew two lines of gathering stitches along seamline of frill, 1.5cm (⅝in) in from pinned raw edges, breaking stitching between each notch. Pull up threads to gather.

8 Fold front cushion piece in half twice and cut a notch in folds. Attach frill evenly, adjusting gathering to match notches and raw edges. Tack into position. See Fig. 8.

9 Open zip. Place back against front cushion, right sides together and enclosing piping and frills. Pin, tack and stitch all round. Trim frill seam allowance to 1cm (⅜in), if using, clip curves and turn cushion cover to right side. Insert pad and close zip to finish.

Always make cushions very plump and well-filled. A skimpily filled cushion cover will look mean, the fabric will crease more easily and it will not be able to perform its job properly, which is to give comfort and support.

~ Frilled flat cushion ~

A small frilled flat cushion with a neat side zip is handy to tie onto any chair.

You will need

1 Flame resistant foam cushion pad 2.5cm (1in) thick by width and depth of chair seat.
2 Main fabric: twice the length of cushion pad plus 1.5cm (⅝in) all round. Allow extra fabric for large prints.
3 Fabric for frill 5cm (2in) deep: 13cm (5⅛in) wide by 2½ times the outer edges of the pad in length plus 1.5cm (⅝in) allowances for joining.
4 Fabric for two ties 1.5cm (⅝in) wide: each 6cm (2⅜in) wide by 50cm (20in) long.
5 Zip the same length as side of pad.
6 Pattern paper.
7 Pins.
8 Thread to match fabric.

To make pattern

1 Cut two pattern pieces to measurements of pad plus 1.5cm (⅝in) all round.

To cut out

2 Set pattern pieces on fabric, following straight grain, allowing for print design and cut out. Cut out frill and tie strips on straight grain.

To sew

3 To sew frill, join fabric strips where necessary on straight grain with 1cm (⅜in) seam allowances pressed open, to form circle of required length. Fold in half lengthways, wrong sides together and matching raw edges. Pin, then divide into four equal parts by folding in half twice and cutting a notch on folds. Stitch two lines of gathering stitches around frill, along 1.5cm (⅝in) seamline, breaking gathering between each set of notches. Pull up gathers, then set frill against right side of front cushion piece, raw edges matching and notches placed at each corner. Adjust gathering, pin and stitch all round.

4 Attach front and back cushion pieces right sides together at opening side, matching raw edges. Stitch for 5cm (2in) down from each corner. See Fig. 1. Tack remaining opening of seam closed, press seam allowances open and insert zip (see Sewing techniques).

5 Sew ties by pressing in 1.5cm (⅝in) to wrong side along each long edge, tucking in short ends to neaten. Fold in half lengthways, wrong sides together. Pin, then stitch along matched folded edges and across neatened ends to finish.

6 Set the middle of one tie at each back corner of cushion (check cushion against chair seat for positions) with its tails pointing inwards towards centre of cushion piece. Stitch across fold of tie and seam allowances. See Fig. 2.

7 Open zip and attach remaining three sides of front and back cushion, right sides together, matching raw edges and enclosing frill. Tack, keeping frill and ties separate, then stitch all round. Clip across corners, turn, insert cushion pad and close zip to finish.

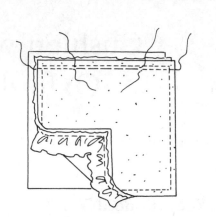

Fig. 1 **Sandwich frill between right sides of front and back cover and stitch, then tack along one side for zip position.**

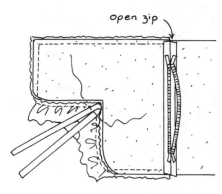

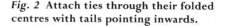

Fig. 2 **Attach ties through their folded centres with tails pointing inwards.**

Cushion with braided Oxford border

An attractive braided border makes this unusual square cushion something special.

You will need

1 Cushion pad.
2 Fabric, twice the length of cushion pad plus 9cm (3⅝in) all round, plus 3cm (1¼in) extra on one side of back cushion piece for zip seam allowances. Allow extra fabric for large prints, up to one pattern repeat.
3 Braid for edging equal to the outside measurements of pad plus 3cm (1¼in) neatening allowance.
4 Zip the width of cushion pad.
5 Pattern paper.
6 Pins.
7 Thread to match fabric.

To make pattern

1 Cut two pattern pieces the measurements of pad plus 9cm (3⅝in) all round. Mark one 'front', then draw line across back pattern, one-third down from top and cut through. Mark each cut 'add 1.5cm (⅝in)' for zip seam allowances.

To cut out

2 Set pattern pieces on fabric following straight grain, allowing for print design and zip allowances, and cut out.

To sew

3 Attach back cushion pieces right sides together at zip opening, raw edges matching, and stitch for 9cm (3⅝in) down each side. Tack remaining opening closed and press seam allowances open.
4 Set in zip (see Sewing techniques).
5 Open zip and attach front to back cushion, right sides together.

Stitch all round, clip corners, turn and press.

6 Lay cushion on flat surface. Pin, then mark line 7.5cm (3in) in from finished edge with pins, tack and stitch all round. Remove tacking and attach braid with slipstitches or by machine so that its inner edge just covers first stitching line, making a small fold at inner edge of braid at each corner to ease round. See Fig. 1.

7 Insert cushion pad and close zip to finish.

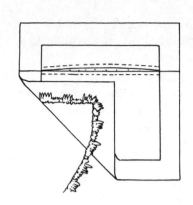

Fig. 1 **The finished cushion cover showing zip position and braid attachment.**

～ Braided cushion ～

This square cushion has sewn-on braid and a plain backing. It is ideal for use with heavyweight fabrics.

You will need

1 Rug, carpet or other heavyweight fabric, size of pad measured both ways plus 1.5cm (⅝in) all round.

2 Lining fabric as above.

3 Cushion pad.

4 Braid, length of four sides of pad plus 3cm (1¼in) neatening allowance.

5 Heavyweight needle and thread.

To sew

1 Neaten round all edges of rug and lining fabric.

2 Set rug and lining fabric right sides together and pin. Using a larger stitch length and looser tension, stitch all round, curving off corners and leaving a gap 20cm (8in) wide in the centre of one side through which to turn. Trim corners around curves and cut wedge shapes evenly around curve of rug fabric seam allowance to remove bulk. See Fig. 1.

3 Turn to right side. Set braid around seamline, tucking in braid ends so they cross over each other into gap seam allowance. See Fig. 2. Slipstitch (see Sewing techniques) all round, attaching to rug fabric at gap. Insert pad and slipstitch gap closed to finish.

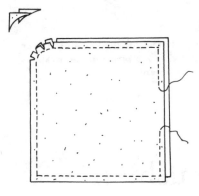

Fig. 1 **Inside of cover showing one curved corner which has been trimmed and notched.**

Fig. 2 **Criss-cross ends of braid and tuck in neatly to conceal before slipstitching closed.**

Make old napkins and scarves into cushion covers. Paisley men's hankies often have darker borders which you can feature as the edges of the cushion.

Piped box cushion

This attractive piped cushion has a curved back designed to fit a wicker chair.

You will need

1 Fabric (see step 1).
2 Contrast bias cut fabric for piping, twice outside measurements of pad plus 1.5cm (⅝in) joining and neatening allowances in length, by 3cm (1¼in) plus circumference of piping in width.
3 Zip, length of back welt pattern minus seam allowances (see step 1).
4 Flame-resistant foam pad.
5 Preshrunk piping cord.
6 Pattern paper.
7 Pins.
8 Thread to match fabric.

To calculate fabric and pad requirements

1 Make pattern of seat shape by laying paper on chair and pencilling around edges. Remove paper, add 1.5cm (⅝in) all round and cut out pattern. Purchase pad to pattern shape minus seam allowances and to required depth, cutting to shape if necessary with bread knife held at right angles to pad. Mark a point one-third of the way down each side of the pad from back curved corners. See Fig. 1.
2 For welt (side) of cover requirements, measure around front of pad from marked point to marked point, then around back from point to point. Cut back and front welt patterns to length of each measurement by depth of pad, plus 1.5cm (⅝in) seam allowances all round, adding 3cm (1¼in) to depth of back welt pattern only. Split back welt pattern in half lengthways to create zip opening. Name each pattern piece, marking seat 'cut two'. These pattern pieces represent fabric requirements.

To sew

3 Cut out all fabric pieces. Cut out and join contrast piping strips (see Sewing techniques) to form two long strips, then wrap contrast piping around each cord length, right side outside, raw edges matching and tack all round, close to cord edge.

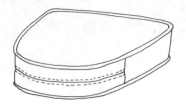

Fig. 1 **Finished box cushion with piping showing position of zip at back.**

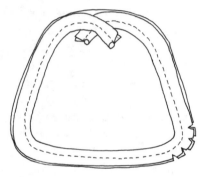

Fig. 2 **Position of piping on right side of seat cover.**

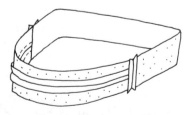

Fig. 3 **Wrong side of cushion welt with zip stitched into back section.**

4 Attach piping around right side of top seat, matching raw edges and curving front corners. Place piping ends to back of cushion, criss-crossing over to neaten, then tack and stitch 1.5cm (⅝in) seam allowances, clipping piping seam allowances at curves to ease. See Fig. 2. Repeat for under seat cover.

5 Pin back welt pattern pieces together along zip opening edge, right sides together, and tack, then stitch in 2cm (¾in) from each side. Press seam allowances open and insert zip (see Sewing techniques).

6 Make up welt by joining front to zipped back welt pieces right sides together at short ends to form ring. Stitch twice for strength and press seam allowances open. See Fig. 3.

7 Pin top seat to welt ring, right sides together, matching raw edges and zip position to side markers. Point ends of piping towards raw seam allowance edges before stitching 1.5cm (⅝in) seam allowances using zip foot. Open zip and repeat for under seat cover. Clip curves where necessary and press seam allowance towards welt. Turn to right side and insert foam to finish.

Upholstery

If you can spare the time, small upholstery projects can make a real difference in completing the decor of a room. It is particularly satisfying if you can restore an old chair or headboard for a fraction of the cost of replacing it.

∼ Buttoned bedhead ∼

You can put new life into an old bedhead by recovering it. Don't forget to place one fabric width centrally and half-widths to each side.

You will need

1 Fabric for front headboard, width and depth of headboard when joined plus allowances all round of 30cm (12in), plus extra for print matching, or measure original and add seam allowances as above.
2 Lining fabric for back headboard, as above.
3 Extra fabric, contrast or self, for buttons.
4 Button moulds, size as originals.
5 Upholsterer's double-pointed straight needle 25cm (10in) long.
6 Scissors.
7 Strong, fine twine.
8 New wadding if necessary.
9 Chalk.
10 Little rolls of waste fabric 3cm (1⅛in) square, for each button.
11 Ruler.
12 Upholsterer's flat-headed tacks.
13 Hammer.
14 Gimp pins (small-headed tacks).
15 Gimp (braid).
16 Copydex.

To prepare bedhead

1 Remove original front fabric and back lining fabric carefully, taking out any tacks and cutting twine ties holding buttons in place. Do not remove wadding unless renewal is necessary. Draw central chalk line down wrong side of old cover. Measure horizontal and vertical distances between buttons. Spread new fabric right side down and draw chalk line down centre, then starting at centre, mark in button positions, reducing all measurements by 5mm (⅛in), since original fabric will have stretched.

To sew

2 Make up buttons with extra fabric, following manufacturer's instructions.

3 Draw a central line down wadding and set fabric right side uppermost over it, matching lines. Thread length of twine through a button and thread needle with both ends of twine. Locate a central button position, thread through top cover and into wadding, passing needle right through to back. Some headboards are made with plywood which will have holes drilled in it at button positions through which you can pass needle, otherwise simply stab needle through webbing and hessian centre to back, pulling button down into hollow and needle out at back. Make slipknot on twine (see Fig. 1), insert a roll of waste fabric between knot and back of headboard to prevent knot pulling through, then tighten knot by pulling one twine end tight. Leave 15cm (6in) twine behind each button back.

4 Continue as above for remaining buttons, completing one diamond shape at a time. Fold pleats formed in fabric downwards, using a ruler to set each pleat in place neatly.

5 When you have set all buttons in place, and pleats are positioned flat, you will find loose fabric on all sides of headboard which would have formed the next set of pleats. Fold this remaining pleat fabric directly to edges, i.e. vertically for top and bottom of bedhead and horizontally downwards for sides, folding pleats over side of bedhead to back frame. Set temporary tacks half-way into frame through fabric, 2.5cm (1in) apart, beginning in the centre of top, then bottom of frame, then each side. Continue to pull fabric and

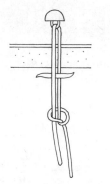

Fig. 1 Making a slip knot.

Fig. 2 Pulling button firmly down to tie off with a reef knot.

pleats tight over to frame back, adjusting tacks where necessary before hammering home. This will take some time but is important to the finished look of bedhead.

6 Pull each button down firmly and tie off securely with a reef knot, see Fig. 2, cutting off twine to neaten. Trim fabric allowance all round to inside edges of tack heads.

7 To attach back lining, firstly mark central line down headboard back, then wrong side of fabric. Position lining matching chalk lines right side outside and folding in raw edges for 1cm (⅜in) set temporarily with tacks, beginning centrally on each side and working outwards as before. Adjust where necessary for taut, smooth backing, then hammer tacks home. Trim fabric allowance to outside edges of tack heads.

8 Fold one end of gimp under and attach at bottom corner of back bedhead, over lining edge, with temporary gimp pin. Glue roughly 30cm (12in) of gimp evenly but not thickly, then press into place, inserting temporary gimp pins at intervals until glue has set. Continue around bedhead to starting point, folding gimp neatly at each corner, setting with gimp pin and tucking raw end of gimp under folded starting edge. When glue is dry, remove temporary pins and insert more pins, hammering home at 10cm (4in) intervals and at corners until they cannot be seen in braid.

~ Chair seat ~

A dropped-in chair seat is a simple recovering project.

You will need

1 Fabric, size of seat measured each way plus 15cm (6in) all round.
2 Lining fabric (ordinary curtain lining or hessian) for bottoming, 2cm (¾in) wider each way than seat.
3 Tacks, 1cm (⅜in) fine-headed.
4 Wadding, if necessary.
5 Chisel, pliers and hammer.

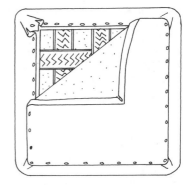

Fig. 1 **Fabric tacked into position on underside of frame.**

To make

1 Remove seat and bottoming from chair by setting chisel under tack head and levering upwards. Pull out with pliers. Remove wadding if worn.
2 Mark each side of fabric and undersides of chair frame at central points. Lay fabric face down on floor and set wadding centrally on top, fluffy side down. Set seat frame over fabric and wadding, aligning central marks.
3 Bring fabric at back of chair seat up and over back edge of frame and attach with tacks set halfway into wood, beginning at centre and working outwards to

Fig. 2 **One corner of finished chair seat folded back to reveal tacks near inner frame edge and position of folds.**

each side, placing tacks 2.5cm (1in) apart. See Fig. 1.

4 Lift front frame to rest on its back edge and smooth fabric over underside of front frame. Pull taut and attach as before. Repeat for each side.

5 At each corner pull fabric up hard and tack at frame corner, see Fig. 2, then fold excess fabric into tiny pleats, trimming away underside of each pleat if necessary.

6 Check that top of seat is smooth and fabric is taut, lifting and repositioning tacks where necessary. Hammer tacks home, then trim fabric allowance to 1cm (⅜in) from tacks.

7 Set lining bottoming centrally against base of seat, turn under 2cm (¾in) so fold covers first line of tacks, and tack as before, pulling fabric evenly taut.

If you are used to recovering dropped-in seats, or are adept with your needle, why not contrast pipe the edges for a very professional finish? You will have to make a pattern of the seat, marking in the edges carefully and adding seam allowances all round. A separate pattern piece will then be required for the sides, stitched into a circle into which you will sandwich the piping, raw edges all together, exactly as for making up a box cushion with piping. Then simply finish off the underneath of the seat as normal. Worth a try.

Fabric-covered wooden screen

This screen is lacquer-painted around its edges, set with fabric and lining for the back, and with neatened gimp (braid) edges. For a more classical, less expensive version, apply round-headed tacks instead of gimp. Details of both methods are given below.

You will need

1 Two sheets medium density fibreboard (MDF), each 183cm (6ft) by 122cm (4ft) by 18mm (¾in) thick.
2 Straight rule and pencil.
3 Drill.
4 Jigsaw.
5 Undercoat.
6 Coach paint or lacquer.
7 Brushes for undercoat and lacquer paint.
8 Brass self-recessing hinges or webbing.
9 Brass screws for fixing hinges.
10 Sandpaper.
11 Medium- to heavyweight fabric, four lengths each 183cm (6ft) long by 61cm (2ft) wide.
12 Lining (curtain lining will do) or contrast backing fabric as above.
13 Flat-headed tacks if using gimp.
14 Gimp (braid) and gimp pins, enough to go round each panel twice or round-headed tacks.
15 Masking tape.
16 Small hammer.
17 Copydex.

To make

1 Mark each fibreboard sheet down its centre with straight rule and cut to make four panels each 183cm (6ft) long by 61cm (2ft) wide. Taking one panel, draw lines 10cm (4in) in from each side to form inner rectangle. Mark down 73.5cm (29in) from each inner top corner, and up same amount from each inner bottom corner and draw lines across panel to form position of central strut dividing large rectangle into two smaller ones. See Fig. 1.
2 Drill corners of each smaller rectangle with drill bit equal to

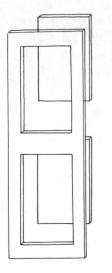

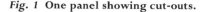

Fig. 1 **One panel showing cut-outs.**

thickness of jigsaw, then saw from each corner to remove two smaller rectangles. Sand all edges and corners thoroughly until very smooth.

3 Repeat for remaining three panels.

4 Apply several coats of undercoat to each panel.

5 Apply lacquer paint to each panel, taking particular care of outside edges and first 5cm (2in) in from edges since this part of panel will be visible when finished. To avoid bubbling, press brush against side of pot to remove excess paint rather than dragging it over rim. Leave to dry thoroughly in dust-free area, then

apply second coat and dry.

6 Mark position of hinges at one side of each outer panel and on each side of two central panels, setting hinges 25cm (10in) in from top and bottom of each panel. Drill and fix, following manufacturer's instructions, being careful to align each panel evenly. See Fig. 2.

7 Take one fabric piece and press 3cm (1¼in) to wrong side all round, only if using round-headed tacks. Mark top and bottom centre points with pins, mark corresponding top and bottom rectangle 'window' centres, then

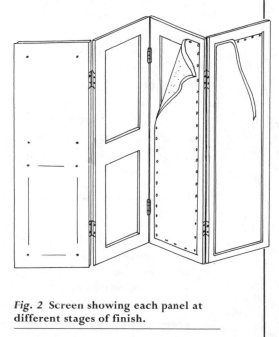

Fig. 2 **Screen showing each panel at different stages of finish.**

attach fabric edges to panel front, matching central points and allowing 3cm (1¼in) of lacquered frame to show all round outside. Tape into position using masking tape and readjusting where necessary, then place temporary tacks or round-headed tacks hammered only halfway in, at centre of top and bottom of fabric, close to edge and work outwards at 2.5cm (1in) intervals, keeping fabric evenly taut. Set temporary tacks at each side as before, adjust tautness, then hammer tacks home carefully, avoiding lacquered frame edges. Repeat for other panel fronts, trimming away excess fabric if applying gimp.

8 If using gimp, fold under one end of gimp and attach to bottom corner of one panel, over fabric edge, with temporary gimp pin hammered only halfway in. Glue 30cm (12in) of gimp evenly but not thickly and set in position up one side of panel. Press into place, inserting temporary gimp pins at intervals and at corners, folding corners neatly as you go. Continue until starting point and turn under 1.5cm (⅝in) to finish, butting up to starting point and fixing with a little glue and gimp pins. When glue is dry, remove temporary pins and insert more pins set at 10cm (4in) intervals and at corners, with heads well hidden in gimp.

9 Apply lining fabric to panel backs as before and set with gimp or round-headed tacks to finish.

Note: Lining fabric could be any contrast fabric edged in different gimp to provide a reversible screen. You could also attach prepared wooden mouldings to outside edges of each panel to cover fabric edges, mitring at corners to create a more ornate version. Gimp would then be unnecessary but fabric would have to be masked off before paint was applied.

Stand a screen in a dull corner or use it to divide a room or hide a washbasin or radiator. A smaller screen could stand on a table against the wall to provide height and interest. Instead of using fabric, you could cover it with photographs of your holidays, cut out and arranged in such a way as to hide the wood beneath.

Lampshades

Lampshade frames are available in all good craft shops so you can choose exactly the size and shape to suit your room.

∼ Firm lampshade ∼

You can use an empire or cone shaped frame for this stylish firm lampshade.

You will need

1 Strutted, straight sided empire or cone shaped frame with dropped pendant fitting.
2 Steel dressmaking pins.
3 Needle, Betweens 5/6.
4 Lampshade tape or soft, unbleached cotton tape 1.3cm (½in) wide.
5 Quick-drying all-purpose glue.
6 Wooden clothes pegs.
7 Scissors.
8 Thimble.
9 Laminated art paper to take pattern size, see below.
10 Selapar or self-adhesive lampshade backing material, size as paper.
11 Matching or contrast velvet ribbon, 1cm (⅜in) wide.
12 Brown paper for pattern.

To make

1 Bind whole frame, or top and bottom if plastic-coated, as follows, allowing about one and a half times length of each strut for binding tape. Beginning at top of frame, place tape under frame and wind round strut, overlapping each edge slightly and pulling tape gently to stretch. Avoid forming any ridges. At bottom of strut, turn frame upside down and wrap tape in figure-of-eight, finishing

Fig. 1 **Lampshade frame showing beginning of binding with knot being pulled tight to outside of frame.**

with a knot pulled tight so tape comes to outside of frame. See Fig. 1. Trim off tape to bottom ring.

2 Bind each strut as above, then bind top and bottom rings, wrapping figures-of-eight around each strut join. Finish as before.

3 Place taped frame on brown pattern paper and beginning at a strut, rotate firmly-held frame slowly, marking roll lines at outside edges of top and bottom rings with pencil on paper, until first strut is reached. Add 1cm (⅜in) seam allowance at one end. See Fig. 2. If art paper and backing material are not large enough, draw only one half pattern inclusive of seam allowance and reverse for other half.

4 Cut out pattern and check fitting on frame, adjusting if necessary.

5 Set art paper right side down on flat surface and pin or tape corners flat. Partly remove backing sheet from adhesive material and position edge over art paper, matching edges. Smooth adhesive material firmly down over art paper, pulling away backing sheet as you work, until whole area is covered.

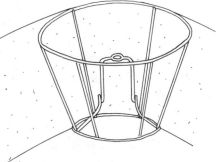

Fig. 2 **Lampshade showing pattern formed by rotating the frame edge.**

6 Cut out lampshade cover and secure to frame with clothes pegs. Sew to tape at top and bottom rings with blanket stitch (see Sewing techniques) in double thread, finishing 5cm (2in) before lampshade cover seamline.

7 On inside of frame, mark off 6mm (¼in) seam allowance with ruler and pencil and trim card to this line. Cut carefully, then glue each edge evenly and press together to fix. Finish stitching at top and bottom rings.

8 Apply velvet ribbon along top and bottom ring edges with glue evenly applied, pressing carefully over stitches to conceal them. Fold in each ribbon edge for 1cm (⅜in) and butt up to neaten, gluing to finish.

～ Pleated lampshade ～

A soft fabric is needed to create the pleated effect on this empire or cone shaped lampshade.

You will need

1 Main fabric, soft sheer material such as silk chiffon, jap or shantung silk or other fabric of natural fibres (which have more 'give'), cut to width of three times circumference of bottom ring by depth of frame plus 12.5cm (5in). A 43cm (17in) lampshade takes between 3–4 widths of fabric, which do not need to be joined.

2 Lining fabric, lightweight and with 'give' i.e. crêpe backed satin, soft fine poplin, cotton lawn. Depth of frame plus 12.5cm (5in) by circumference of bottom ring of frame plus 12.5cm (5in), cut so straight grain runs from top to bottom of frame.

3 Lampshade tape or soft, unbleached cotton tape 1.3cm (½in) wide.

4 Steel dressmaking pins.

5 Strutted, straight sided empire or cone shaped frame with dropped pendant fitting.

6 Sharp scissors.

7 Needle, Betweens 5/6.

8 Hard pencil.
9 Lampshade braid, circumference of top and bottom rings plus neatening allowances of 1.5cm (⅝in).
10 Pins.
11 Thread to match fabric.

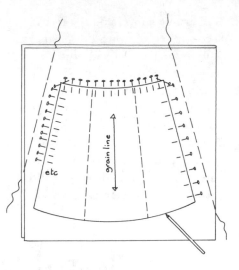

To sew

1 Bind whole frame following instructions given in 'Firm lampshade' steps 1 and 2.
2 To attach lining to frame fold lining fabric double, right sides together and set on one half of frame with straight grain running from top to bottom centre of half-frame. Place pin at each corner of half-frame and pin down each side strut from top to bottom at 2.5cm (1in) intervals, placing pins with points facing inwards and smoothing away fullness. Pin round half-frame at top and bottom rings, placing pins 2.5cm (1in) apart as before. See Fig. 1.
3 Tighten fabric at top and bottom rings to ease out any wrinkles, then complete pinning at side struts, placing pins at 1.3cm (½in) intervals.
4 Draw faint pencil line down

Fig. 1 **Folded fabric pinned into position against half-frame.**

side struts to mark sideseams, extending line 1.3cm (½in) above and below top and bottom rings. Tack 1.3cm (½in) to outside of side struts, through both layers of fabric to hold. See Fig. 1.
5 Remove pins and lining and machine stitch down each pencil line, stretching fabric slightly while stitching. Trim seam allowances to 6mm (¼in) and press closed.
6 Turn lining right side out and fit over frame so seamline and allowances run directly behind side struts. Pin at top and bottom, making sure seams do not slip out

of place. See Fig. 2. Tighten fabric carefully so lining fits taughtly over frame. Oversew (see Sewing techniques) lining to frame with double thread onto outer taped edge of top and bottom rings, working from right to left. Leave both seam allowances untrimmed.

7 Take one width of main fabric and decide on width of pleat (6mm (¼in) for finer fabrics to 1.3cm (½in)), then turn in one raw edge for pleat depth along grainline and set in position at side strut, allowing at least 7.5cm (3in) of spare fabric below bottom ring. Pin at top and bottom. Fold next pleat in position on grainline and set at bottom ring, leaving a small space between pleats since more fabric will have to be accommodated at top ring because of shape of shade. Continue pleating and pinning along bottom ring to next strut, then set pleats with pins at top ring, keeping each pleat on straight grain and in line with bottom pleat.

8 Pin next section, using same number of pleats. Continue until all sections are completed, joining fabric by overlapping at end of first set of pleating with new pleat, joining if possible at strut position. Slip end of last pleat

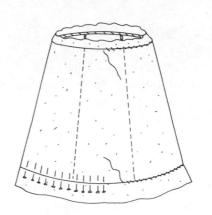

Fig. 2 **Lining fabric set in position on outside frame.**

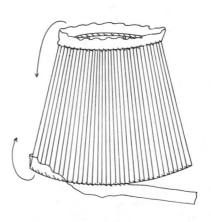

Fig. 3 **Lining being folded over outside neatened edges of pleating.**

under first one to finish.

9 Oversew (see Sewing techniques) pleats to binding at top and bottom rings using double thread, making sure they are evenly taut.

10 Trim top and bottom pleats to stitching line, then neaten lining at top and bottom by folding over neatened pleat edges to outside of frame (see Fig. 3) and oversewing (see Sewing techniques) in single thread, using one small, then one normal-sized stitch. Trim seam allowances to stitching lines.

11 Set braid against top ring of shade to cover all stitches, beginning at strut position and turning in 1.3cm (½in) to neaten. Sew in position, taking tiny alternate stitches at top and bottom of braid to produce a zig-zag effect. Do not stitch through lining. Turn in braid as at beginning to finish, slipstitching (see Sewing techniques) closed at butted edges. Repeat for bottom ring.

Tablecloths

It can be much cheaper to make your own tablecloths. And you'll have them exactly the right size and avoid the irritation of them being just too short or too long.

~ Square fringed tablecloth ~

This square cloth can be made with or without a lining, and has an attractive decorative fringe.

To calculate fabric requirements

1 Measure across tabletop and add twice required drop to this measurement. If resulting square is wider than fabric, it will have to be joined. Tablecloths are never joined in the middle: a whole width of fabric is positioned down centre of table; further widths (usually a half-width is enough) fall to each side. See Fig. 1. Fabric requirements will therefore double, plus extra

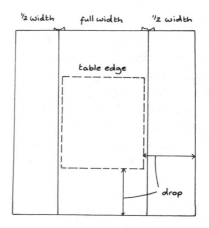

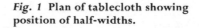

Fig. 1 **Plan of tablecloth showing position of half-widths.**

fabric equal to print repeat measurement. Subtract seam allowances from both main and side strips of fabric before adding 1.5cm (⅝in) all round for a lined cloth, or 7.5cm (3in) all round for an unlined one.

2 Lining fabric, as main fabric measurements but without print repeat allowance.

3 Fringing, measurement of chalkline mark (see step 4) plus 10cm (4in) neatening allowance.

4 Pins.

5 Thread to match fabric.

To sew

1 Cut central fabric panel to length, then fold remaining length in half lengthwise and cut down fold. Remove selvedges.

2 Join main panel to side panels of tablecloth, matching print (see Lined curtains, To sew, step 23), right sides together and stitch. Press seam allowances open (for an unlined cloth these should be neatened). Trim off any overlapping lengths of side panel fabric formed when prints were matched.

3 Repeat steps 2 and 3 for lining, not allowing for print matching.

4 To apply fringing, mark a line 15cm (6in) in from outer edge of tablecloth with chalk and lay fringing along it, beginning at one corner and pinning as you go. At second corner, fold heading of fringing to make right angled turn, then continue all round. Tuck under raw edges and slipstitch (see Sewing techniques) carefully at both top and bottom of fringe heading so it lays flat. Slipstitch all round tablecloth, or machine stitch round twice, stitching at both top and bottom of fringe heading.

5 Set lining against main fabric, right sides together and matching raw edges. Pin, then stitch all round, leaving an opening in centre of one side 30cm (12in) wide through which to turn. Trim corners, turn and press. Slipstitch remaining gap closed and press again to finish. For an unlined cloth, turn under 1cm (⅜in) all round edges and press. Turn under 6.5cm (2⅝in) again to wrong side, pin and stitch all round by hand or machine, mitring corners (see Sewing techniques).

Add to the size of a too-small or unloved tablecloth by attaching a border mitred at each corner and sew napkins to match.

∼ Circular tablecloth ∼

A bound edge gives a distinctive finish to this lined cloth.

You will need

1 For main fabric, measure across widest part of tabletop and add twice drop required. No seam allowances are necessary, since edges are bound. Add a further 15cm (6in) to measurements for a drape of 7.5cm (3in) onto ground if required. If fabric is not as wide as measurements it will have to be joined. Refer to instructions for joining widths in Square fringed tablecloth, allowing for print repeat. See p. 98.

2 Binding fabric cut on cross, 10cm (4in) wide for 2.5cm (1in) binding by length of circumference plus neatening allowances of 10cm (4in) and extra fabric for bias joins (see Sewing techniques). 100cm (39¼in) of 122cm (48in) wide fabric will provide 888cm (348½in) of 10cm (4in) wide bias binding, 50cm (19⅝in) of fabric 444cm (174½in) binding.

3 Lining fabric as for main fabric but without print repeat allowance.

4 Pencil, string and pins.

5 Thread to match fabric.

Set a glass top over a circular tablecloth to protect it, or use a smaller, less precious cloth over the first one which can be easily removed for washing.

To sew

1 Follow steps 1 to 3 in Square fringed tablecloth. Fold main fabric into quarters, right sides inside and press, matching raw edges and seamlines.

2 Divide total diameter measurement of cloth in half, tie length of string to pencil, measure along string to length arrived at above and put pin through it at this point. Set pin firmly at central point of folded fabric and with string taut, draw an arc from side to side. Cut along this line. Repeat for lining.

3 Set main fabric against lining, wrong sides together and pin and tack all round raw edges.

4 Join binding on bias (see Sewing techniques) to achieve necessary length, then follow Narrow curtain binding, steps 2 and 3 to finish.

Fill a large shallow bowl or basket with large coloured glass balls matching the colours in your room. Use tissue paper in a matching colour crumpled up under any objects in a bowl and they will look brighter. Arrange small pots of crocuses or polyanthus in a large, flat basket; you can put them in the garden when they've finished flowering. Or, make an arrangement of dried flowers for the centrepiece of a coffee table. Big shells are great for bathrooms and a large glass storage jar could be filled with pebbles in interesting shapes from the beach. Free, too!

Miscellaneous

There are all sorts of small projects you can undertake to brighten up your home. Many of these are ideal for the beginner to test their skills before embarking on some of the larger projects.

～ Napkins ～

If you wish, you could make smaller napkins out of narrower fabric exactly as below, dividing the fabric length vertically and following steps 1 and 2 below.

You will need

1 Fabric, 68.5cm (27in) square. Fabric 135/138cm (53/54in) wide will make two napkins per width, taking 68.5cm (27in) fabric, so eight napkins would take 274cm (108in) fabric.
2 Thread to match fabric.

To sew

1 Cut out required number of squares, then press in 1.5cm (⅝in) twice along each edge to wrong side, mitring corners (see Sewing techniques).
2 Slipstitch (see Sewing techniques) across mitres, then stitch close to inner folded edge and press to finish.

～ Quilted tablemats ～

You will need

1 Main fabric, 30.5cm (12in) by 41cm (16in) rectangle. Fabric 135/138cm (53/54in) wide will make three mats per width, taking 30.5cm (12in) fabric.
2 Contrast or backing fabric as above.
3 Contrast bias cut binding fabric, 6cm (2⅜in) wide by 158cm (62in) long for each mat, plus extra for bias joins. 50cm (19⅝in) of 122cm (48in) wide fabric will produce 740cm (290½in) of 6cm (2⅜in) wide bias binding, enough for four mats.
4 Synthetic wadding, 1cm (⅜in) thick by mat size.
5 Pins.
6 Thread to match fabric.

To sew

1 Cut main fabric, contrast backing and wadding to size. Draw in diagonal quilting lines on fabric both ways, beginning from corner to corner and working outwards at 2.5cm (1in) parallel intervals. Lay backing fabric wrong side uppermost with wadding on top, then set main fabric right side up (Fig. 1) and tack all round, then across centre both ways. Tack further lines 2.5cm (1in) apart from top to bottom and from side to side, working outwards from centre.
2 Using a longer and looser tensioned machine stitch which has been sampled on spare fabric, stitch marked diagonal lines, beginning at a corner-to-corner line and working outwards.
3 Cut contrast binding on cross to measurements given above,

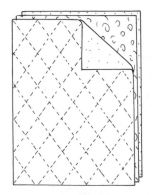

Fig. 1 **Wadding sandwiched between main and backing fabric.**

joining on bias (see Sewing techniques). Press seam allowances open, then press 1.5cm (⅝in) to wrong side down one long edge of strip. Pin unpressed long edge right sides together against main fabric, matching raw edges and turning under 1cm (⅜in) at beginning short raw edge of binding. Stitch all round 1.5cm (⅝in) in from edge. Press binding and seam allowances away from mat, fold over to wrong side and set pressed edge over stitching line. Slipstitch (see Sewing techniques) into place, mitring corners (see Sewing techniques) and slipstitching across binding join. Press to finish.

∾ Oven glove ∾

You will need

1. Main fabric, two squares of 30cm (12in) each.
2. Lining fabric as above.
3. Contrast bias cut binding fabric, one strip 6cm (2⅜in) wide by 30cm (12in) long and second strip 6cm (2⅜in) wide by 10cm (4in) long.
4. Synthetic wadding, 2cm (¾in) thick as above.
5. Pins.
6. Thread to match fabric.

To sew

1. Cut out paper pattern. See Fig. 1.

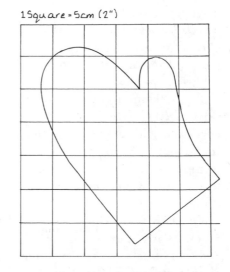

1 square = 5cm (2")

Fig. 1 **Paper pattern for oven glove.**

2 Chalk in diagonal quilting lines both ways on main fabric squares, marking in corner to corner lines and continuing in 2.5cm (1in) parallel lines to each corner. Cut two squares of fabric, lining and wadding to size, using pattern. Set lining square right side down, cover with wadding and top with main fabric, right side up. Tack all round, then beginning in centre, tack down and across glove at 2.5cm (1in) intervals, working outwards in each direction. Repeat for other square.

3 Check tension and stitch length on spare fabric for a looser, longer stitch then stitch along diagonal marked lines in both directions across fabric squares. Cut out front and back glove pieces, reversing pattern to achieve a 'pair'.

4 Pin back and front glove right sides together, matching raw edges and sew 1cm (⅜in) seam all round glove, leaving opening unstitched. Neaten seamline and turn, clipping into curve of thumb to ease.

5 On short bias strip, press under 1.5cm (⅝in) at each long side and fold in half again, then stitch along matching folds to form loop tab. Join contrast strips for longer length on bias (see Sewing techniques), press seam allowances open, then press one long edge of binding strip 1.5cm (⅝in) to wrong side. Attach unpressed long edge of strip right side to outside main fabric of glove at opening raw edge, beginning at back and turning under 1cm (⅜in) at short end to neaten. Pin, then stitch 1.5cm (⅝in) seamline all round opening. See Fig. 2. Press binding and seam allowances away from glove,

Fig. 2 **Attaching binding to oven glove.**

turn to inside and set pressed edge against stitchline. Insert raw ends of loop tab into back seam allowance of glove, matching raw edges and stitch securely, then slipstitch (see Sewing techniques) pressed binding edge all round to close. Press to finish.

~ Frilled apron ~

You will need

1 Fabric, 83cm (32¾in) by 60cm (23⅝in) for apron and ties, 83cm (32¾in) of 122cm (48in) wide fabric.
2 Contrast fabric for frills and pocket, 65cm (25½in) of 122cm (48in) wide fabric.
3 Pattern paper.
4 Pins.
5 Thread to match fabric.

To make pattern and cut out

1 Draw out main apron pattern as shown in Fig. 1 and add 1.5cm (⅝in) seam allowances all round. Draw out pocket pattern, adding 1.5cm (⅝in) seam allowance to curved edge and 5cm (2in) across top. Cut out patterns.
2 Cut out apron in main fabric and pocket in contrast. Cut frill

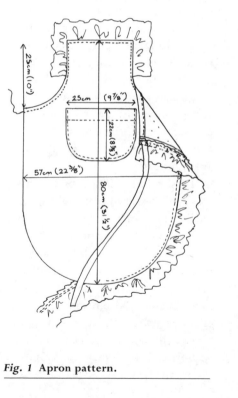

Fig. 1 Apron pattern.

strip 345cm (135½in) long by 13cm (5⅛in) wide, and small frill strip, 60cm (23⅝in) by 13cm (5⅛in). Cut two waist ties 50cm (19⅝in) long by 10cm (4in) wide and one neck tie, 55cm (21⅝in) long by 10cm (4in) wide.

To sew

3 Neaten curved edge of pocket, fold under 2.5cm (1in) twice at top straight edge, press and stitch close to inner folded edge from side to side. Press under 1.5cm (1in) round neatened edge from corner to corner and set centrally in position on apron, matching neatened pocket top to level of underarm points. Pin, then edgestitch around curve, close to pressed edge. Stitch again 1cm (⅜in) in from first stitching line, around curve.

4 To sew frills, join fabric strips where necessary on straight grain with 1cm (⅜in) seam allowances pressed open, to form required lengths. Fold in half lengthways, wrong sides together and stitch across short ends to neaten. Turn to right side and pin long raw edges together. Mark central point along frill, then stitch two lines of gathering 1cm (⅜in) and 1.5cm (⅝in) in from raw edges,

breaking stitching at pin marker. Pull up loosely.

5 Mark central points at bottom and top of apron with pins. Attach large frill to apron, right sides together, matching raw edges, central pin points and beginning and ending 1.5cm (⅝in) below underarm corner points. See Fig. 2. Pin, adjust gathers then stitch all round 1.5cm (⅝in) in from raw edges.

6 Repeat frill attachment for small frill, beginning and ending 18cm (7in) down each side.

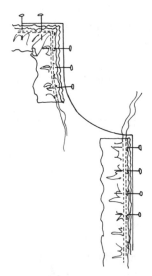

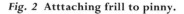

Fig. 2 **Atttaching frill to pinny.**

7 Neaten all round edges of pinny, neatening frill and apron seam allowances together. Press frill seam allowances and underarm seam allowance of 1.5cm (⅝in) to wrong side, clipping curves to ease where necessary. Edgestitch all round pressed edges of pinny on right side. Stitch again 1cm (⅜in) in from first line of stitching and through all seam allowances, all round apron, pivotting needle at corners to turn.

8 To make ties, press 2.5cm (1in) to wrong side along each long side of tie and press in half lengthways again, wrong sides together. Unfold raw short ends, fold in for 1cm (⅜in) and repress to neaten. Edgestitch each waist tie down long side and across one pressed-in end, then edgestitch along long side only of neck tie.

9 Attach unstitched short end of each waist tie to wrong side of apron at underarm point (see Fig. 1) and stitch across twice, following existing stitch lines, to secure. Attach neck tie at one side of apron top, then adjust length on other side and stitch as above to secure. Press to finish.

∽ Pole end cover ∽

You will need

1 Fabric, see calculations.
2 Lining as fabric.
3 Pattern paper.
4 String.
5 Pins.
6 Thread to match fabric.

To make pattern

1 Measure from centre of ball top to neck and add 5cm (2in) seam allowance for radius. Fold pattern paper in half twice, tie one end of string to pencil and mark off radius measurement with drawing pin. Set pin at double fold corner and mark an arc from side to side of folded paper. Cut out around marked line.

To sew

2 Unfold pattern and cut one circle of fabric and one of lining. Pin one over other, right sides together and stitch 1cm (⅜in) seam allowance around outside edges, leaving gap through which to turn. Clip curves and turn to right side. Press pole end and slipstitch (see Sewing techniques) closed gap.

3 Run two lines of gathering stitches round outside of circle, 3cm (1¼in) and 4cm (1⅝in) in from edge. Draw up gathers and set over ball end of pole. Tie to secure. See Fig. 1.

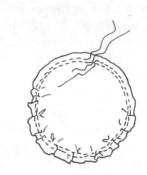

Fig. 1 **Drawing up gathers of cover.**

⁓ Chairback cover ⁓

You will need

1 Main fabric, see below for measuring.
2 Contrast backing fabric, as above.
3 Contrast tie fabric, two lengths each 100cm (39in) by 18cm (7⅛in) wide making a total of 36cm (14¼in) of fabric 100cm (39in) wide.
4 Pins.
5 Thread to match fabric.

To sew

1 Measure chairback from middle of top horizontal strut to planned bottom of cover and add 11.5cm (4⅝in) hem and seam allowances. Measure its width from outside centre of left side strut to centre of right side strut and add 3cm (1¼in) seam allowances. See Fig. 1.

2 Cut one main fabric and one contrast backing fabric to these measurements. Cut two strips for ties.

3 Pin main fabric cover piece to backing fabric piece, right sides together and matching raw edges and stitch 1.5cm (⅝in) in from edge across top and down each side. Neaten seam allowances separately and press open.

4 Turn in 2.5cm (1in) to wrong side at opening raw edge, press and turn in same again. Stitch close to inner folded edge, or slipstitch (see Sewing techniques) hem. At top corners of cover, fold diagonally so seamlines come together and stitch across at right angles, the depth of chair back wood. See Fig. 2.

5 To make ties, fold one strip in half lengthways, right sides together and matching raw edges and stitch down complete length, leaving a gap of 12.5cm (5in) through which to turn. At each short end stitch a diagonal line to

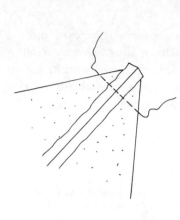

Fig. 2 **Fold cover diagonally and stitch across corners.**

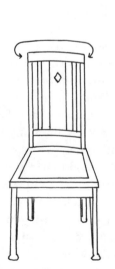

Fig. 1 **Measuring width of chair.**

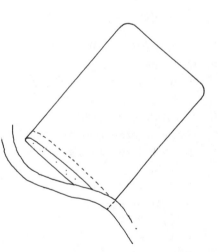

Fig. 3 **Finished cover showing position of ties.**

close. Trim corners, turn and press, then slipstitch (see Sewing techniques) closed turning gap. Attach centre of each tie to base of cover at sideseam (see Fig. 3)

and stitch from top to bottom and through sideseam to secure. Set cover over chairback and wrap ties in around chair struts and out again to tie in bows.

Fabric wall hanging

You will need

1 Original fabric for hanging.
2 Lining fabric, size of hanging minus turning allowance, plus 2.5cm (1in) all round.
3 Interlining, size of original fabric.
4 Hessian backing fabric, close weave, weight to match weight of hanging, size as hanging minus turning allowance.
5 Small brass rings for hanging.
6 Curtain weights, chain or coins.
7 Chalk.
8 Drill and bit to match hook size.
9 Rawlplugs.
10 Screw hooks, brass.
11 Pins.
12 Thread to match hanging fabric.

To sew

1 Back original fabric with interlining by first laying fabric right side down and marking lockstitch chalk line down centre from top to bottom. Mark further lines outwards to each side, about 20cm (8in) apart. Mark corresponding lines down centre of interlining, then to each side.
2 Set interlining over fabric, matching chalk lines and raw edges, pin down length of interlining and fabric at central line and fold back interlining at pins. Lockstitch (see Sewing techniques) interlining to fabric, beginning and ending just within turning allowance of fabric.
3 Repeat pinning procedure at next chalkline and lockstitch, working outwards both ways until interlining attachment is complete.

4 Repeat steps 1 to 3 for hessian attachment so that raw edges of hessian touch foldline of fabric all round.

5 Fold over turning allowance all round fabric edge to wrong side and pin, inserting chain weight or single coins along inside lower folded edge of hanging. Catch chain or individual evenly spaced weights into position with a few handstitches along inner folded edge, then mitre corners (see Sewing techniques) and tack folded edge into position all round.

6 Keeping fabric/hessian right side downwards, mark central chalkline down hessian and further lines 23cm (9in) apart on each side. Repeat for wrong side of lining fabric, then set lining over hessian, chalklines matching and raw edges of lining overlapping folded fabric edges evenly all round.

7 Pin, then sew lockstitching lines as before, working outwards from centre but allowing 5cm (2in) free all round sides.

8 Fold under lining seam allowance round all edges to about 1.5cm (⅝in) from folded fabric edge, depending on depth of fabric seam allowance. Pin then slipstitch (see Sewing techniques) all round. Press flat carefully.

9 Attach rings evenly to lining at top back of hanging. Set hanging in position against wall, mark in horizontal hook positions and drill wall as marked. Insert rawlplugs and screw hanging hooks into place. Hang to finish.

❧ Picture bow ❧

You will need

1 Fabric, see below.
2 Small ring.
3 Tape measure.
4 Picture hook.
5 Pins.
6 Thread to match fabric.

To calculate fabric requirements

1 Measure length of tail required from central bow point to top centre of frame, double this measurement and add depth of frame. Fold tape measure into half bow loop required and add this amount, opened out (here 25cm (10in)), to measurement. Double measurement for total finished length and add 2cm (⅝in) for seam allowances.

2 Cut strip to total length by double width required plus 2cm (⅝in) for seam allowances (here cut 17cm (6¾in) wide for 7.5cm (3in) wide bow/tail). Cut a 15cm (6in) square of fabric for bow knot.

To sew

3 Fold long strip in half lengthways, right sides together and stitch diagonally across each end in opposite directions, then down long side, taking 1cm (⅜in) seam allowances and leaving gap of 15cm (6in) through which to turn. Trim diagonal short ends to 1cm (⅜in) seam allowances, trim corners, turn and press. Close opening with slipstitches (see Sewing techniques).

4 Fold fabric square in half one way, right sides together, stitch down matched long raw edges, fold to form tube and turn to right side.

5 Mark centre of long strip with pin, then mark length of bow

loop on each side with pins. Fold loops into position (see Fig. 1) and secure with handstitches through centre, leaving tails loose.

6 Roll seam allowance of knot to centre back of tube, wrap one raw end around back of stitched bow at knot position and pin. Wrap

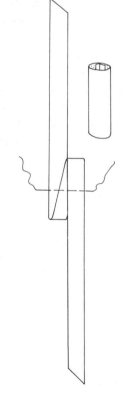

Fig. 1 **Loops being stitched into position at centre of strip.**

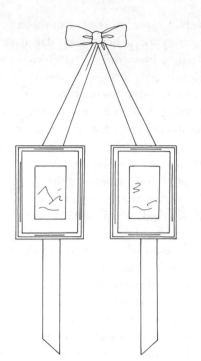

remaining end around back, folding under to neaten and forming one or two downward facing plump pleats in the centre of each bow loop. Stitch pleats lightly and invisibly to hold, then slipstitch (see Sewing techniques) knot into position at back to form a rounded shape.

7 Stitch ring to centre back knot and hang from hook, threading each tail under a frame to fall below it. See Fig. 2.

Fig. 2 **The finished look – why not try dropping both tails behind a single picture as an alternative?**

～ Gilding a picture frame ～

You will need

1 Old frame.
2 Fine wet or dry sandpaper.
3 Wood filler if necessary.
4 Oil-based paint for base coat, chestnut, dark maroon or black.
5 Clear mid-gloss polyurethane varnish.
6 2.5cm (1in) decorator's brush.
7 2.5cm (1in) artist's brush for varnish.
8 Three small saucers.
9 Three shades of gilt powder, dark, medium and light.
10 Cleaning and polishing rags.
11 Three little pieces of velvet,

small sponges, soft artist's brushes or sticks with cotton wool rolled around one end.

12 Small tube artist's oil colour, raw or burnt umber or sienna.

13 White spirit for cleaning brushes.

To prepare surface

1 Fill any cracks or missing sections with wood filler and rub smooth with wet or dry sandpaper. Rub remaining frame areas gently and dust clean, then wipe over carefully with damp rag. Allow to dry.

2 Apply oil-based paint over entire frame with decorator's brush and leave to dry completely.

3 Wipe over dried frame with damp rag to remove any dust, touching frame as little as possible. Dip artist's brush halfway into varnish and press against side of pot to remove excess and avoid bubbles, rather than over rim. Varnish entire frame. Leave to dry in undisturbed corner until just tacky.

4 Tip one shade of powder into each saucer, being careful not to breathe on it or inhale. Take a tiny amount of powder onto

velvet piece, dust off excess on spare paper, then tap or dab over area to be covered, blotching lightly onto frame. Repeat with each powder colour randomly, leaving blotched areas of base coat showing through and overlapping powder in places. Take less rather than more powder for each application, adding gilding bit by bit rather than overdoing it.

5 If liked, wrap another velvet piece around finger and dipping in one powder, remove surplus and rub in tiny circular motion on raised parts of frame to highlight them.

6 Leave varnish to dry completely in dust-free area, then wash over with warm soapy water on rag to remove surplus powder. Dry thoroughly.

7 Mix more varnish with a little artist's oil colour and apply as before to frame with artist's brush, applying more in recesses of frame and less over raised areas. Leave to dry, then rub down with sandpaper and polish with soft cloth to finish. Clean brushes.

Don't be afraid to frame little pieces of embroidery, tapestry or patchwork – in fact anything which you enjoy looking at.

～ Stencilled cupboard doors ～

You will need

1 Carbon paper.
2 Black felt-tip pen.
3 Oiled stencil board.
4 Cutting board.
5 Stanley knife.
6 Buntlac or other acrylic spray paint such as car bodywork retouching paint, in cans.
7 Old newspapers.
8 Masking tape.
9 Cleaning rags.

To paint

1 Mark out evenly spaced grid on original design and grade up or down by increasing or decreasing grid size accordingly. See Fig. 1. Draw chosen design onto stencil board in pencil, then felt-tip pen, transferring from original with carbon paper sandwiched between design and board. Make sure to cut 'bridges' within the design to strengthen stencil board. See Fig. 1.

Add a decorative veneer strip of the type used in marquetry around the edges of uninteresting wooden cupboard doors. Don't titivate anything antique, though, or you may destroy its value.

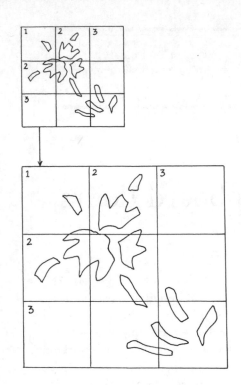

Fig. 1 **Increasing the grid size of your chosen design to suit the position of the stencil on the cupboard door.**

2 Set stencil board onto cutting board with masking tape, allowing 5cm (2in) spare board all round design. Cut round pen marks smoothly, turning cutting board towards you when going round corners in order to get an unbroken line. Trim off any rough edges carefully.

3 Clean and thoroughly dry cupboard doors to be stencilled measuring planned position of stencils with tiny pencil marks at each corner of cut-outs.

4 Attach several small rolled pieces of masking tape to wrong side of stencil, then set in position on door. Mask off whole surrounding area with sheets of newspaper, then shake the paint can and holding it level with stencil and at recommended distance, spray lightly backwards and forwards. Leave paint to dry for a few minutes, then carefully remove stencil and set in next position. Clean stencil occasionally to remove excess paint.

Walls

Using a simple border can enliven a plain room, without the need to redecorate completely. For simplicity, choose a wall-paper border to suit the existing decor. Or you can try some simple stencilling.

∼ Stencilled border on wall ∼

A stencilled border can brighten a plain wall. This one is executed in two colours, but you can choose a single colour if you wish to keep it simple.

You will need

1 Carbon paper.
2 Black felt-tip pen.
3 Oiled stencil board.
4 Cutting board.
5 Stanley knife.
6 Quick-drying paint such as artist's acrylic paint mixed with water or emulsion, or poster paint.
7 Two stencil brushes.
8 Masking tape.
9 Cleaning rags.
10 Two paint saucers.

To paint

1 Mark out evenly spaced grid on original design and grade up or down by increasing or decreasing grid size evenly. See Fig. 1. Stencilled cupboard doors. Be sure to begin and end at one design run so there is no break in design when border is joined up. Draw chosen design onto stencil board in pencil, then felt-tip pen, transferring from original with carbon paper sandwiched between design and board and drawing in

one colour area only. Make a separate board for the second colour area.

2 Set stencil boards on cutting board with masking tape, allowing 5cm (2in) spare all round design. Cut smoothly round pen marks, turning cutting board towards you when going round corners in order to get an unbroken line. Trim off any rough edges carefully.

3 Line up two stencil boards so that design fits together and trim board edges so they are even. Cut a notch on each side of design, through both boards at once and line up on wall with small pencil mark at 'V' of notch for matching design.

4 Clean wall to be covered, mark position of border along the wall, measuring up from floor or skirting board with small chalk markings to check position of border is level. Then, attaching small pieces of masking tape to back of first colourway to be stencilled, set in position on wall, using markers.

5 Prepare and mix paint to chosen colours, dip tips of bristles into saucer to take up very small amount of paint, then rock flat end of brush backwards and forwards on spare paper to distribute paint evenly. Apply brush to stencil design in a 'pouncing' motion as though rubber stamping, working from outside inwards to centre. Leave paint to dry for a few minutes, then remove board carefully and set further along border line, placing carefully in position using pencil markers as before. Continue around wall, bending board at corners of wall so design continues unbroken, and cleaning stencil occasionally with rag to remove excess paint.

6 At end of colourway sequence, clean stencil and brush carefully, then repeat around wall in remaining colourway. Clean equipment before storing stencil flat.

~ Wallpaper border ~

Borders can be applied at ceiling height to emphasise good proportions, at chair rail height to add interest to a bleak wall, around doors, windows and at picture rail or skirting board height.

It is worthwhile borrowing or buying a small length of border paper to make sure its effect is pleasing before purchasing. If this is not possible, draw a mock-up of the design and colour it in, then set against the wall for effect. Borders work best when they contain in muted shades some of the colours already in the room and can successfully pull together disparate colours to give a finished look. Try placing above a dado or picture rail, around the architraves of doors and windows to emphasise them or at ceiling height to lower a disproportionately high ceiling. Very stark rooms can be much softened by the use of borders and of course there are many

wallpapers with matching borders available which take the agony out of choosing. Where an existing wall is colourwashed, try using a border with toning background to give new life to the colour; it may save having to redecorate the room.

Apply your border with usual manufacturer's wallpaper paste, following packet instructions for mixing. If adding a border at chair rail height, make sure to mark its correct horizontal position before beginning by measuring up from floor or skirting board and marking at intervals with chalk along proposed line of border. Bend border around corners so design stays unbroken and when joining, be sure to match design, cutting border ends on bias if possible. When turning around right angles on a flat wall, mitre corners as for fabric (see Sewing techniques, Figs 1 and 2 on p. 134).

Beds

Here are a few projects to try in the bedroom to give a professional touch to your new decor, or to give a lift to the existing decoration.

～ Lined bedspread ～

You will need

1 Fabric (see steps 1 and 2 below).
2 Contrast bias fabric for binding, twice length and width of finished bedspread measurements plus seam allowances for joining, cut 8cm (3⅛in) wide for 2cm (¾in) wide binding. 100cm (39¼in) of 122cm (48in) wide fabric will produce 1036cm (406¾in) of bias binding, 50cm (19⅝in) of 122cm (48in) fabric 518cm (203⅜in) of binding and so on.
3 Lining as fabric.
4 Large plate.
5 Pins.
6 Thread to match fabric.

To calculate fabric requirements

1 Draw plan of bed and add the following measurements. Measure width and length of bed with normal bedclothes in place. Allow 15cm (6in) extra fabric for any tuck-in at front edges of pillows and for 20cm (8in) drop behind them. Decide on drop measurement around foot and sides of bed, usually to the floor unless there is a valance, when drop comes to below top of valance gathering. See Fig. 1.
2 For total width of bedspread, add width of bed to twice drop. For total length, add length of bed complete with tuck-in and pillow

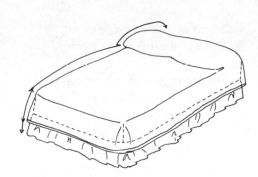

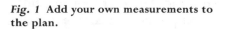

Fig. 1 **Add your own measurements to the plan.**

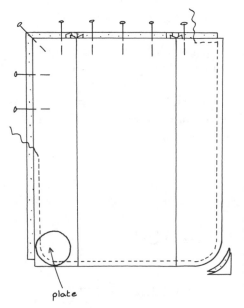

plate

Fig. 2 **Main fabric and lining being attached, wrong sides together, in readiness for bound edging.**

drop to once foot-of-bed drop. No seam allowances are required. As it is unlikely that fabric will be as wide as requirements, it will have to be joined. One whole width of fabric is always placed down centre of bed and half widths joined at each side, joins falling at edges of bed if possible. See Fig. 2. To total measurements (usually twice total length) add one pattern repeat allowance for matching pattern. To calculate this, simply measure from the top of one pattern to the same point on the next one.

To sew

3 Cut out central fabric width, beginning at start of pattern repeat. Cut second fabric width, fold fabric in two lengthways and cut down middle. Remove selvedges.

4 Join central width to side panel half widths, matching pattern by pressing side of panel to be joined to wrong side along seamline and placing against central width so pattern matches. Pin, then ladderstitch (see Sewing techniques) across join. Fold fabric right sides together and stitch from top to bottom. Repeat for other side.

5 Repeat for lining, omitting print matching instructions. Press all seam allowances open.

6 Set fabric over lining, wrong sides together and matching raw edges and seamlines. Pin down seamlines, wrap main fabric back against pins and lockstitch each seamline from top to bottom (see Sewing techniques). Fold fabric back into position and pin all round, matching raw edges. Set curved edge of plate at each corner of foot of bedspread, mark round and cut off two corners. Tack all round bedspread edge. See Fig. 2.

7 Join binding strips on bias (see Sewing techniques) where necessary to achieve required length around sides and foot of bedspread. Join separate length for top. Press one long edge of each strip 2cm (¾in) to wrong side.

8 Beginning at one side of top of bedspread, attach unpressed long top binding edge right sides together and raw edges matching across top of bedspread and pin, then stitch 2cm (¾in) seamline. Press binding away from bedspread, fold over to wrong side and set pre-pressed edge on top of stitching line. Pin, then slipstitch (see Sewing techniques) into place. Repeat for sides and foot of bedspread, tucking under 2cm (¾in) to neaten at each end and taking small folds into prepressed edge of binding at rounded corners when slipstitching. Slipstitch neatened binding edges at top of bedspread to close and press to finish.

~ Frilled valance ~

You will need

1 Fabric for frill (see step 1).
2 Lining or sheeting fabric for bed top.

To calculate fabric requirements

1 Remove mattress and measure width and length of bed, adding 1.5cm (⅝in) to sides and foot of bed for seam allowances and 5cm (2in) for top neatening. If lining fabric is not as wide as bed top, it will have to be joined. A complete width of fabric is placed down bed centre, with panels to each side. Calculate an extra 1.5cm (⅝in) for each seam allowance. See Fig. 1.

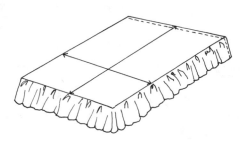

Fig. 1 **Add your own measurements to the plan.**

2 Measure drop to floor. Add 1.5cm (⅝in) at top and 6.5cm (2⅝in) at bottom edge, for total depth of frill. Multiply length of bed measurement by four and add to twice width of bed measurement. Divide this total by width of fabric, adding seam allowances of 1.5cm (⅝in) to each side of seamline join where necessary and one pattern repeat per width if matching pattern, to make up total frill length. Add 6.5cm (2⅝in) at each short end.

To sew

3 Pin top lining sections if necessary, right sides together, stitch, neaten and press seam allowances open. Press under 2.5cm (2in) twice along top and stitch close to inner folded edge to neaten.

4 Join valance strips with 1.5cm (⅝in) seam allowances. Match patterns by pressing one side of seam allowance at each fabric width join to wrong side. Set over next width to be joined until pattern is matched. Pin, ladderstitch (see Sewing techniques), wrap pressed fabric to wrong side and stitch down seamline. Repeat for other joins, neaten all seam allowances and press open. Press under 1.5cm (⅝in), then 5cm (2in) at each short end to wrong side and machine stitch close to inner folded edge or slipstitch (see Sewing techniques). Repeat for lower valance edge and press.

5 Measure twice bed length from each neatened short end of valance and mark with two pins at raw top edges. Divide the three sections formed into two and mark again. Mark foot and sides of top lining section in half with pins along raw edges. Stitch two lines of gathering 6mm (¼in) apart on each side of 1.5cm (⅝in) seamline, along raw edge of valance between pin markers. Draw up gathering sections and set right sides together against top lining section, matching pin markers to breaks in gathering. Adjust gathering, pin and stitch. Neaten seam allowances together and press away from top section to finish.

～ Half-tester ～

Draped fabric is lined, bound and gathered onto an angled bracket which is topped with a pole end cover. (See p. 107)

You will need

1 38cm (15in) bracket (a shelving bracket or similar will do).
2 Main fabric (see step 3).
3 Lining fabric (see step 3).
4 Contrast fabric for binding (see step 4).
5 Wadding for bracket and pole end.
6 Main and lining fabric for pole end (see p. 107 for instructions).
7 Fabric tape measure and pencil.

To place bracket

1 Mark wall at a height of about 175cm (65in) from top centre of mattress. Drape tape measure from marked central point down over bedside and note angle of tape from point with pencil mark. Attach bracket to wall following manufacturer's instructions and setting bracket base at marked angle from central point. The base will then be concealed by fabric drape.
2 Wrap wadding around bracket to achieve a plump, rounded

effect about 5cm (2in) in diameter. Stitch, then wrap with any odd fabric and stitch to finish, forming a lining cover for bracket.

To calculate fabric requirements

3 Drape tape measure from top centre of padded bracket, down over side of bed to floor. To this measurement add 30cm (12in) for floor drape when tied back, plus 10cm (4in) hem turning allowance. Multiply by two for total fabric length, one fabric width (usually 135/8cm (5¾in)) wide. Lining requirements will be as main fabric width plus 10.5cm (4¼in) in length.
4 Contrast bias fabric for binding, finished length of main fabric plus allowance for bias joins and 2.5cm (1in) neatening allowance at each end, cut 10cm (4in) wide. 50cm (19⅝in) of 122cm (48in) wide fabric will produce 444cm (174⅝in) of 10cm (4in) wide bias binding.

To sew

5 Cut main fabric and lining to requirements along fabric length and remove selvedges. Cut off strip 10.5cm (4¼in) wide across lining width to make channel for bracket and set aside.
6 Press 4cm (1⅝in) to wrong side along one long main fabric edge. Press 10cm (4in) to wrong side at each short end for hemlines. Press 2cm (¾in) to wrong side along one long lining edge and set 2cm (¾in) in from pressed edge of main fabric, wrong sides together to form a border. Pin, then slipstitch from side to side, trimming lining at each hem end to match folded hemline. Fold under side of hem to mitre (see Sewing techniques) at lining edge only, then turn lining to wrong side to form a hem, leaving 2cm (¾in) main fabric border. See Fig. 1. Slipstitch across lining hemline at each end to neaten.
7 Press main fabric and lining flat, trim lining to match raw edge of main fabric along remaining long side and tack along whole length.
8 Join contrast binding strips on bias (see Sewing techniques) to length of fabric plus 2.5cm (1in) at each end. Press seam allowances open, then press 2.5cm (1in) to wrong side along one long edge of binding strip. Pin unpressed long edge to raw tacked edges of half-tester, right

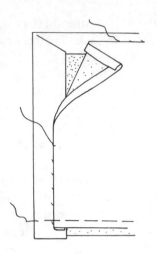

Fig. 1 One end of the half-tester showing position of lining.

Sewing techniques) along binding length and at each folded in end to neaten. Press.

9 Fold finished half-tester in half lengthways to find centre, mark across width on lining side with chalk. Press long raw edges of bracket channel lining fabric to wrong side by 1.5cm (⅝in). Draw a chalk line down centre of wrong side of channel, and set against lining side of main fabric so chalk lines match. Turn in twice at each end to neaten, stitch across, then reset channel against fabric, matching chalklines. Pin, then stitch close to folded edge down each side to finish.

10 Gently push plain long edge of half-tester onto covered bracket through channel, gathering up fabric until binding edge is on. Make pole end cover (see p. 107), stuff with wadding and attach to bracket end, tying threads to secure.

sides together and matching edges, folding under 2.5cm (1in) at each end to neaten. Stitch from end to end. Press binding away from half-tester, wrap over to wrong side and set folded pressed edge to stitchline. Slipstitch (see

Cut and sew the outer edges of worn sheets into new pillowcases, Oxford (flat) bordered or housewife-style (completely plain) and edged with broderie anglaise trimming. Or stitch them with contrasting colour thread to match an existing duvet cover or sheet.

～ Oxford-edged pillowcase ～

You will need

1 Fabric, for pillowcase 75cm (29½in) long by 50cm (19⅝in) wide, 105cm (41¼in) of fabric 120cm (48in) wide. See Fig. 3.
2 Pins.
3 Thread to match fabric.

To sew

1 Cut front pillow piece 89cm (35in) long by 60cm (23⅝in) wide and back pillow piece 99cm (39in) long by same width.
2 Press under 1cm (⅜in) on front pillow piece at one short end to wrong side. Fold pressed edge back to right side by 5cm (2in) and stitch 1cm (⅜in) seam allowances down each side. See Fig. 1. Turn back to right side, then press under 5cm (2in) again and tack along inner folded edge.

3 Press under 1cm (⅜in) twice to wrong side of back pillow piece at one short end and stitch. Press neatened edge 20cm (8in) to wrong side and tack down each side.
4 Attach front to back pillow piece, right sides together, matching raw edges and stitch across bottom then up each long side, taking 1cm (⅜in) seam allowances and clipping seam allowance to ease on front piece where border begins, at each side. See Fig. 2. Trim closed seam allowance corners, turn case and press.
5 Complete flat border stitching by firstly tacking around two long sides and closed end of pillowcase, 5cm (2in) in from pressed edges. Following tacking line, stitch a close zigzag stitch around four sides of case, being careful not to include back opening fold in stitching line. See Fig. 3. Press to finish.

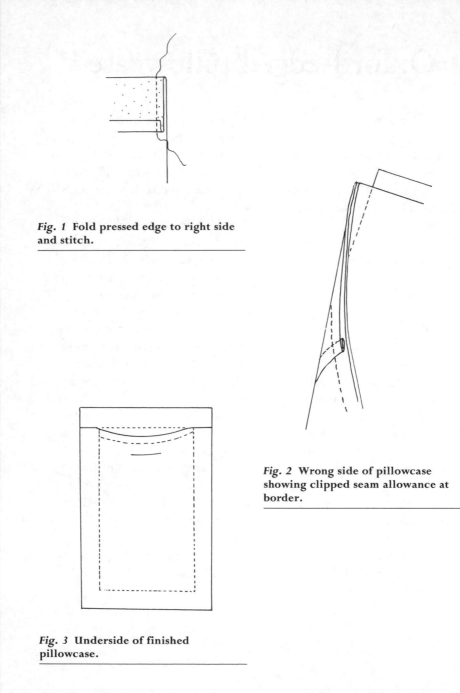

Fig. 1 **Fold pressed edge to right side and stitch.**

Fig. 2 **Wrong side of pillowcase showing clipped seam allowance at border.**

Fig. 3 **Underside of finished pillowcase.**

Lace-edged pillowcase

You will need

1 Fabric for pillowcase 75cm (30in) by 50cm (20in), fabric 169cm (66½in) long by 51cm (20in) wide.
2 Lace or broderie Anglaise, 51cm (20in) wide by any width.

To sew

1 On one short end of all-in-one case, press under 5mm (¼in) twice to wrong side and stitch. Press a further 15cm (6in) to wrong side, unfold and attach lace to right side of case with its prettiest edge just overlapping pressed line. Stitch across lace at top and bottom. Refold flap and tack down each side. At other short end, press under 1cm (⅜in) then 2cm (⅝in) and stitch.
2 Fold case right sides together so pressed short edges meet. Pin, then stitch 1cm (⅜in) seamlines down each long edge. See Fig. 1. Neaten seam allowances and turn to right side. Press to finish.

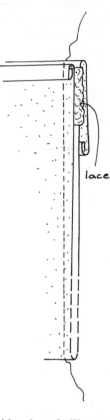

lace

Fig. 1 **Inside edge of pillowcase before turning.**

Make a lined bedspread, sandwiching interlining between printed fabric and lining. Pin, then handstitch with decorative stitches to quilt around some of the printed areas on the bedspread at roughly even intervals between stitching areas. Flowers and leaves, for example, can take on a three-dimensional look with this technique, and it is much easier to do on a large area of fabric than trying to quilt a whole bedspread on your sewing machine. Alternatively, you could appliqué sections of the print on top of the existing fabric, which could give much the same effect.

Sewing Techniques

～ Bias strips ～

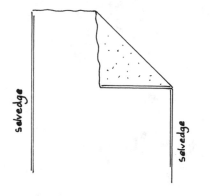

Fig. 1 Folding right-angled corner of fabric to form bias marker.

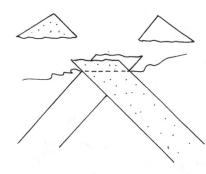

Fig. 2 Join bias strips by placing right sides together at right angles. (Stitch across, trim excess fabric and press seam allowances open.)

Cutting bias strips

1 Find bias of fabric by folding selvedge over on cross so selvedge lies parallel to crossways grain. Cut along fold to form marker. See Fig. 1.

2 Draw bias lines in chalk following cut marker line to width required and cut.

Joining bias strips

Place two strips right sides together on bias, stitch, trim seam allowances to 1cm (⅜in) and press open. See Fig. 2.

～ Blanketstitch ～

Secure thread at top left edge.
Insert needle 6mm (¼in) below
top edge, point upwards and loop
thread over behind point. Draw
thread up so it lies at top edge
and repeat.

～ Herringbone stitch ～

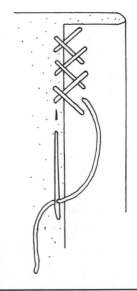

Hold folded hem edge towards
you, then starting from the left,
bring thread up through hem
3mm (⅛in) from edge. Move
6mm (¼in) diagonally to right
across hem edge, taking small
stitch from right to left just below
hem edge. Stitch across hem edge
6mm (¼in) diagonally to right
and take small stitch to left. Bring
thread diagonally to right and
take small stitch to left, below
hem edge. Repeat, forming
crossed stitches along hem edge.

~ Ladderstitch ~

To join matched fabric patterns, insert needle into wrong side of folded pressed edge and bring out at fold edge. Take small stitch across join, bringing needle out 2cm (¾in) below insertion point on flat side. Take another small stitch back across join into fold, bringing needle out 2cm (¾in) further down fold. Repeat.

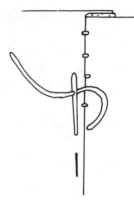

~ Lockstitch ~

Stitch through folded lining edge and curtain fabric at right angles to fold, picking up two or three threads only. Wrap thread over needle to produce loop and insert into folded lining edge and curtain fabric 5cm (2in) down fold. Repeat.

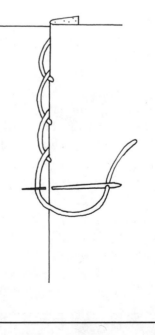

~ Mitred corner ~

Turn in two sides along foldline and press. Mark with pins where inner raw edges touch. See Fig. 1. Unfold and fold again diagonally from pin to pin. See Fig. 2. Press, remove pins and slipstitch closed. If making double folds, trim away excess fabric from point before slipstitching.

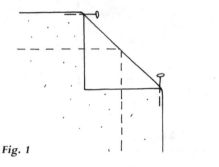

Fig. 1

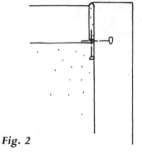

Fig. 2

~ Oversewing ~

Working from left to right, take thread over raw fabric edge to wrong side, bringing needle through fabric from back about 3mm (⅛in) from edge each time.

❦ Setting in zip ❦

1 Measure zip and mark position and length on tacked seamline. See Fig. 1.
2 Set zip face down in position with zip teeth centred over seamline. Pin then tack to set. On right side, stitch 6mm (¼in) away from teeth down one side, using zip foot. Pivot needle at bottom corner, stitch across zip base and pivotting needle at other corner, stitch across top to finish. Press. See Fig. 2.

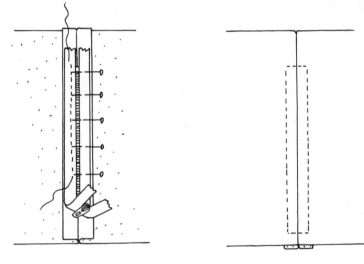

Fig. 1

Fig. 2

～ Slipstitch ～

Hold inner folded hem edge towards you, then starting from the right, make tiny stitch in main fabric close to folded edge. Do not pull thread through, but insert needle into folded edge close to first stitch and bring out 6mm (¼in) to left. Pull thread through and repeat.

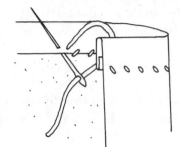

~ List of Suppliers ~

Inexpensive furnishing fabrics:

John Lewis Group (prints, wovens, plains, linings and trims). Branches in:

Aberdeen
Bristol
Edinburgh
High Wycombe
Kingston
Milton Keynes
Peterborough
Watford
Welwyn
London
Brent Cross
Oxford Street
Peter Jones, Sloane Square
Bainbridge, Newcastle
Bonds, Norwich
Caleys, Windsor
Cole Bros., Sheffield
Heelas, Reading
Jessop & Son, Nottingham
Knight & Lee, Southsea
George Henry Lee, Liverpool
Robert Sayle, Cambridge
Tyrrell & Green, Southampton

Material World (prints, plains and linings). Branches in:

Bath
Bury St Edmunds
Edinburgh
Glasgow
Kingston-upon-Thames
London
Battersea
Chelsea
Southfields

Newbury
Tunbridge Wells

Ian Mankin Ltd (wovens)
109 Regent's Park Road
London NW1

Other good sources for furnishing fabrics include bin ends in department stores such as Liberty (London and branches), warehouse sales, house clearance sales, auctions, markets and jumble sales.

Lampshade materials:

For lampshade frames, fabrics, Selapar stiffening and trims:

Selfridges (London)

Stencils:

Carolyn Warrender
Stencil-itis
91 Lower Sloane Street
London SW1

If you live outside London, all of the above London suppliers will supply by mail order.

~ Index ~